SINGLE MOTHERS RAISING SONS fills a definite need for thousands of single moms. . . . Dr. Reed offers not theory or pop psychology, but common sense tested in a "laboratory" called the single parent family. The book is realistic and gutsy. . . .
SINGLE MOTHERS RAISING SONS reads like a conversation with a trusted friend. The reader will take away a sense of "if she can do it, I can too."
In an era of "you can't be a good enough parent," Bobbie Reed debunks the notion of failure. Single moms *can* parent great sons. Bobbie Reed's book is must reading not only for single parents but also for ministers, educators, and people who care.

Harold Ivan Smith, D.Min.
Author of *No Fear of Trying* and
Director of Tear Catchers

To Sandy with love, [signature] 1989'

SINGLE MOTHERS RAISING SONS

Bobbie Reed, Ph.D.

THOMAS NELSON PUBLISHERS
Nashville

Published in Nashville, Tennessee, by Thomas Nelson, Inc., and distributed in Canada by Lawson Falle, Ltd., Cambridge, Ontario.

Printed in the United States of America.

Scripture quotations are from THE NEW KING JAMES VERSION of the Bible. Copyright © 1979, 1980, 1982, Thomas Nelson, Inc., Publishers.

Library of Congress Cataloging-in-Publication Data

Reed, Bobbie.
    Single mothers raising sons / Bobbie Reed.
      p. cm.
    ISBN 0-8407-3113-2 (pbk.)
    1. Children of single parents—United States. 2. Child rearing—
—United States. 3. Mothers and sons—United States. 4. Single
parents—United States. I. Title.
HQ777.4.R44   1988
649′.132—dc19   88–1688
                                    CIP

3 4 5 - 91 90 89 88

*To Kim Johnson, with love,
in acknowledgment of his sweet spirit,
creative ideas, committed ministry,
and unfailing affirmation.*

Contents

Acknowledgments

My experiences, as well as those of the other women I have known raising sons alone, are behind the concepts in this book. The research included both reviewing the current literature on parenting and the single parent experience and interviewing psychologists, single parents, adults raised by single parents, pastors, children, divorce attorneys, custody attorneys, and counselors. I am grateful for the valuable contributions of time and personal sharing all of these have made to this book.

Chapter

1

FEARS
I Can't Raise a Son Alone!

I'll never forget the day I sat in the counselor's reception room waiting my turn to go inside his office to pour out my hurts and anger at having to cope with an impending divorce, because my husband no longer wanted to be married. I struggled to hold myself together, but tears kept leaking out. The pain was so great I didn't think I could bear it.

All of a sudden the realization hit me with the shock of a physical blow. After the divorce I would be a *single parent! I couldn't do it!* My sons were only four and six. What did I know about raising sons alone? I had never been a little boy!

I panicked. How was I going to support all three of us on my meager salary? How was I going to teach them all they had to know? Was I wise enough to cope? Countless questions blurred in my head. I was sure I couldn't do it.

But I did.

The next ten years as a single-again mother were

full of laughter and tears, highs and lows, fun and fears. Sometimes all of these occurred in just one day. Many times I felt I was on an emotional roller coaster ride full of unexpected turns and twists.

Like the time Mike (age ten) won a diving award and I was so proud I felt as if I were Mother of the Year. Then the next day he was suspended from school for misbehavior, and I felt as if I were a total failure!

And how could I forget the time I took the boys to Northern California to see the giant redwoods and our car died right in the middle of the tree you can drive through. Cars stacked up behind us for a mile while we spent an hour trying to figure out how to get our car up a thirty-five-degree incline!

There were tough times financially when making ends meet took extraordinary effort and long hours of overtime. There were tough times emotionally when we found ourselves at the family counselor's office, struggling to hold together as a family. There were nights when I paced the floor both angry and scared because my fifteen year old had broken his curfew and hours when I sat up late devising new ways to challenge the boys to do better in school or in real life situations.

There was joy: special holidays; close, cuddly times, just the boys and me; unexpected moments of honesty and shared feelings; flashes of maturity, hinting of what the boys were becoming.

For the first six years I had full custody of both sons. Then the older chose to live with his father, and a couple of years later the younger decided to go there also. I've been a custodial and a noncustodial single parent and have known the joys and pains of both roles.

I write as a fellow learner, for I am still growing into the kind of parent and person I want to be. I know that I could never have survived some of our experiences with my sanity intact had I not had the Lord's help. My parents brought me up with a strong, unshakable faith in God and His miraculous power. I learned as I grew into adulthood that God loved me enough not only to send His Son to save me but also to care about my daily walk, struggles, and triumphs. I can't count the number of times I've cried out to God for help, for wisdom, claiming James 1:5 as my personal promise: "If any of you lacks wisdom, let him ask of God." He promised wisdom to those who came to Him asking in faith. And for me, asking is a daily occurrence at times.

Through being a single parent, I've learned more about my own relationship with God. When I agonized over a poor choice one of my sons had made, I would often turn to God with the sudden realization that He must sometimes feel the same way about some of my choices. In the last twelve years, as a consultant for single adult ministries, I have met with, talked to, shared with, and counseled hundreds of women raising sons alone. Some of these women were divorced, some widowed, and others unwed. Still others were married but were actually raising sons alone because of a husband's physical absence (in the military, in prison, or at work away from home) or emotional absence (physically present, but providing no help).

In my ministries and through my personal experiences, I have noticed two major themes or concerns that women raising sons alone experience. First, there is a concern about how the boys will develop their sexuality. This issue is complex and a bit scary for us women, considering that we were never little boys. We wonder if we will know what to say and do. We want to teach our sons to be the kind of men we want them to become, rejecting the homosexual lifestyle, learning to treat women the way we think women should be treated, growing up to fulfill the manly role as we define it.

The second concern has to do with values. We each have a set of values that we believe to be important and that we want to pass on to our sons. Our values are beliefs that trigger attitudes and behaviors. We want our sons to grow up to be honest, to work hard, to be caring individuals so we can be proud of them and so they will be successful in life. Yet all too often, our sons don't seem to find those characteristics attractive, at least in their growing-up years. At times we despair of their chances for success.

What's a mother to do?

The message of this book is one of encouragement. While it is full of practical ideas and suggestions for teaching values and sexuality, it does not leave the responsibility for your sons' choices on you. The best you can do is teach, train, set a good example, discuss, provide role models, and then turn your sons over to God. After all, they are His children also, and He cares about how they grow up. So you must learn to trust in His power, not only when yours begins to wane but also when you are feeling strong.

You can make it! You can do it! And you can even enjoy it!

FOUR TYPICAL RESPONSES TO BEING A MOM WITH SONS

There are many different responses to being a single parent. No one feels the same way all of the time. Often we experience several conflicting emotions at the same time. But there are four basic responses to single motherhood.

Type One: *"I Can't Do Anything!"*

I found that I felt this way whenever I had tried my best and everything seemed to be going wrong. If I planned a nice couple of days off to be with the boys and they didn't want to do anything with me, I felt unloved and inept. When I tried to put together a bike for Christmas (Why don't they come assembled?) and the pedal screw got stripped because I twisted it the wrong way, I felt stupid and inclined to quit. When the budget wouldn't stretch far enough to cover things the boys really wanted, I felt inadequate. But these times became fewer and farther between as I gained confidence that I was doing the best I knew how and that most of the time I did okay.

A mother experiencing this response may feel helpless, discouraged, and depressed; give up easily, appearing dependent or weak; not enjoy family times; sleep a lot; be nonassertive; not have a strong supportive group of friends; blame others; or have very few house rules for the children.

The basic beliefs behind this feeling may be:

- I am not a capable person.
- I have been abandoned, so I am worthless.
- Life is unfair, so why try?

- I cannot cope.
- I am a failure.
- I have no control over my life.

When the mother is feeling this way, the sons tend to respond accordingly. They experience a loss of self-esteem and display their inadequacies; they have little self-control; they learn to be manipulative and play on the guilt of the mother. They become expert at taking advantage of the parent.

Type Two: *"I'll Do It or Die!"*

Most of the time during my early years as a single mom, this was my basic approach. I was convinced that I had to do it all. Who else was there to do it? I got up early to pack lunches, clean house, do chores, and catch my breath.

As soon as the boys were old enough to get off to school by themselves, I would go in early to work overtime for extra money and to keep my evenings free to be with them. Of course, I left everything ready for their breakfasts, little notes telling them I loved them, and all of those extra touches that are great, but that take planning and energy—energy I began to run out of as I met myself coming and going. Sure, I was home in the evenings, but I was often too tired to be much company. Finally I began to set realistic expectations for myself and for the boys so our lives could settle into a more livable routine.

Some women respond to the challenge of single parenting by showing their determination to conquer any obstacle. They are compelled to work, work, work, and feel guilty if they sit down to relax. Even though they are chronically tired because of being physically and emotionally drained, they usually feel very good about themselves and what they've accomplished. These moms appear strong, harried, and rushed, and they also have frequent headaches, backaches, tired feet, troubled sleep, and other stress symptoms. Because they operate in high gear most of the time, they are almost always able to squeeze in one more task if necessary and they don't say no easily to requests from others.

Yet these moms tend to be assertive and perhaps a bit aggressive, particularly if their schedules are interrupted. They set absolute rules for their children, and when the children fail to follow the rules or live up to their pace, these moms may become critical and angry.

Women who behave as described usually believe the following:

- I must be a good parent.
- I can/must do everything by myself.
- I dare not fail.
- I must maintain control of everyone and everything.
- No one must suspect I sometimes feel scared or like giving up.
- If even one thing goes wrong, it is a disaster.

Children typically respond to the do-it-or-die approach by letting their mothers do all of the work. They learn that if they procrastinate long enough, do the job poorly, or too slowly, Mom will step in and quickly handle the task herself. A second response is to comply with new rules for a short time, while the pressure is on, but, when Mom moves on to other priorities, they begin to slide. Why? Because Mom probably won't have the time or the inclination to retrace her steps and enforce the rules. Also the children sometimes feel pushed, rushed, resentful, rebellious, or insecure because "Supermom" is a hard act to follow.

Type Three: *"I'm Surviving!"*

We all fall into this approach from time to time. I found that my writing deadlines always seemed to coincide with the boys' extra activities, ones they needed my help on or to be driven to. Of course, that's also when the refrigerator decided to give out, the plumbing clogged, and the car wouldn't start. The worst months were September through December. Getting the boys back to school, handling birthdays, Halloween, Thanksgiving, and Christmas just about depleted the budget and my energies and patience each year. Every New Year's I resolved to take it easy next year. But next year things would be very nearly the same!

Single moms in the survival mode may feel overwhelmed sometimes but okay at other times. They may appear courageous or frazzled or both. But they have learned to acknowledge their inabilities to meet everyone's expectations all of the time, so they try to meet the needs they can. As they experience highs and lows, these moms laugh a lot (sometimes a bit hysterically) and fluctuate between assertion and nonassertion, depending on the situation and their energy levels. They find that no is frequently their first answer, but too often they can be talked into a yes. They change the house rules too frequently, based on the situations, their feelings, and their energy levels.

Sometimes they encourage and affirm the children, but sometimes they yell at them or criticize and blame them.

A survival-oriented parent is often operating on these beliefs:

- I think there's hope, if I can just hang in there.
- I just take one day at a time, because I can't face any more than that!
- Just when I think that things are on an even keel, I can expect them to fall apart.
- Things will settle down someday, I hope.
- Surely one day I will be repaid for surviving and have peace and quiet and the whole house to myself.

The children will probably respond by testing Mom's limits frequently to see what the rules are today, taking advantage of her rough days to get their own way, and being confused about what is acceptable and what isn't. On the other hand, they will also learn flexibility!

Type Four: *"I'm Doing Okay!"*

This last approach to being a single mom is the one that makes the most sense but is not always the easiest to adopt. For me it took constant checking on myself to ensure that I was looking at parenting in the appropriate light.

First, I reminded myself that children are a gift from God (Ps. 127:3) and that they are people, not my possessions. I made a list of ways I was attempting to train up my sons in the ways they should go, per Proverbs 22:6. When I felt inadequate, I checked my list. If I was doing everything on the list and I couldn't think of anything else to do, then I reassured myself that I was doing my best.

Next, I made a list of the ways God has promised to help children without fathers and women without husbands. I found so many promises I cannot list them here (see Appendix A for scriptures that can help).

The third thing I learned to do was to compare my feelings and experiences with friends who were in a similar situation to mine. Their feedback helped me maintain a proper perspective of the daily ups and downs of parenting alone.

The single mom with a positive self-image and a high level of self-esteem will probably feel good about her parenting role and will accept the fact that there will be times when things are out of control. She has learned when to say no to the demands of others, to be fairly assertive, and to prioritize expectations and goals. She makes time for herself in addition to family times and accepts the limitations of her time, energy, and abilities. She is reasonably even tempered (with some highs and lows), has fairly consistent family rules, and usually encourages and affirms her children.

The I'm-Doing-Okay mom believes:

- Nobody's perfect.
- I'm doing the best I know how.
- This too shall pass.
- In the final analysis, the children will make their own choices.
- I am an important person as well as a parent.

Her children tend to respond by growing toward maturity (at their own rates, of course), accepting themselves, and testing the limits whenever possible. And she knows some of them will grow up and succeed in life, while others may not.

SINGLE PARENTING IS SCARY!

"The thought of being a single parent can be frightening!" Kathy explained. "When I was a little girl playing dolls, I always pretended there was also a daddy in the family. I didn't plan on growing up, getting married, having a son, and then raising him alone! I'm afraid. What if I can't do it?"

Kathy is not alone in her fears. The single parents I've counseled with listed several reasons for experiencing fears: inadequacy, criticism, loss of the children (a psychological or emotional loss as well as the physical loss of custody), loneliness, and rejection. All of the fears expressed can be summed up into one big *fear of failure*. When asked what *failure* meant, every mother had her own definition.

Fear of Inadequacy

Self-doubt can plague a mother raising a son alone. *How can I accomplish all of the housekeeping chores, be a twenty-four-hour-a-day parent, and still maintain my sanity?* she thinks. *Who will provide the male role models for the boys?*

The underlying difficulty here is overload: task, emotional, or responsibility. (See Appendix C for resources for coping as a single parent.)

There will be days when the noise level in your apartment is deafening, the living room looks like the town dump, your favorite vase has just been broken, and one of your children says, "You don't love me! You always take Larry's side!" You may want to resign. For such a day, I recommend two Bible verses. Deuteronomy 33:25 says, "As your days, so shall your strength be." Galatians 6:9 promises, "Let us not grow weary while doing good, for in due season we shall reap, if we do not lose heart."

I remember joking with my friends about when could we expect the harvest? There were times when it felt a long time coming, and I had to cling to those verses with everything I had. It was great to remember that I could never use up God's promises or His strength. There was a new supply every morning.

Fear of Rejection

Tanya confessed, "Richard wants to go live with his father. I don't think I can take it! What if he likes his stepmother better than he likes me?"

In spite of the overload of trying to do it all, all by themselves, most mothers still prefer to retain custody of their sons. The thought that a boy might go to his father is frightening. In a later chapter we deal with this issue.

Fear of Loneliness

"Being alone is not necessarily bad; being *lonely* is the pits!" Sara says.

Most people would agree. You can be alone and not be lonely and be married or with friends and feel lonely. A person is lonely to the extent that he/she perceives a lack of *essential* emotional or psychological support. When you are lonely, it is more than someone's presence or company you desire, it is an affirmation of your self-worth. You've probably noticed that when your self-esteem is high, you are less lonely than when you are not feeling positive about yourself.

Therefore as a safeguard against persistent loneliness, you will want to develop a healthy, positive self-concept. Learn to be independent. Practice assertive techniques that will help you meet your needs. Set reachable goals and celebrate your achievements in those areas. Identify and use your gifts and talents to reach out to help others. Develop a supportive network of friends who can provide the love and attention you need. Reach out to someone who may be hurting even more than you are just now and give love and affirmation. It is in giving that you receive.

Fear of Criticism

Parenting is one area in which we don't feel we can afford to be a failure. Society and even the church seem to forgive failure in business, marriage, finances, school, and even criminal actions once the prison term has been served. But no one forgives poor parenting.

Therefore, most moms work hard at trying to live up to everyone's expectations. But it doesn't work for several good reasons. Everyone has a different set of expectations. And who is to say who is right? Because the expectations of others tend to be idealistic and unrealistic, each mother needs to decide how she will function as a parent and what the house rules will be.

When someone does criticize what you are doing or

how you are handling your sons, don't let it devastate you. Remember that your style is uniquely yours. Listen to the input, but evaluate whether or not there is merit for you at this time. If so, plan to make changes. If not, file the remarks away for future reference when the comments might apply. Learn to be assertive and self-confident in your choices and decisions.

Another secret to coping with criticism is to be sure that when you set your priorities and goals that you seek God's input. Ask God what things you should be working on at this time. Make a list. Develop a plan to focus on top priorities and to reach your goals, and stick to your plan. If someone disagrees with your priorities and goals, it just means that they don't happen to have God's insight into what is important for you at this time. In essence, they aren't criticizing you, they just don't have all of the facts. Another good reason to get God's input is so that you will be headed in the right direction to becoming conformed to the image of His Son as we are instructed to be in Romans 8:29. Why trust in our own knowledge or insight, when we can depend on His?

ARE YOU A SUCCESS OR A FAILURE?

Take a few moments to make a list of what you honestly expect of *yourself* as a parent and another list of what you expect of your *son*. You may be surprised at how long the lists are. Next look at each item and decide if it is realistic. Cross off or rewrite unrealistic expectations so that you end up with practical lists. Keep them handy for reference the next time you feel depressed or a failure as a parent. Chances are you are doing better than you feel you are when measured against *realistic* expectations.

The truth is, there are no criteria for evaluating the success or failure of a person in the single parent role. People establish their own standards for success. When these standards are achieved, people *feel* successful. When they fall short of these expectations, people *feel* that they have failed. Therefore, people who set unrealistic goals have two choices—lower their expectations or consider themselves a failure.

Sometimes the parent-child relationship doesn't work well in spite of the best efforts of both parties. Sometimes we do fail. In those cases, people must remember that *failure as a single parent is not failure as a person!*

You will fail at times. That is a given. In 1 John 1:10 we are told that if we say we don't sin (fail), that we are not being truthful. But, 1 John 2:1 goes on to say that if we do fail, we have an advocate with the Father, our Lord Jesus Christ. He understands and covers our failures with His blood, so that as we confess those sins, we are forgiven (1 John 1:9). What a promise! We do our best, but when we fail, we are forgiven. What a relief!

Being forgiven is easy. Accepting forgiveness, though, can sometimes be a problem. We don't forgive ourselves or accept the fact that God has forgiven us, so we continue to beat ourselves with guilt over our real or imagined failures. We need to be tenderhearted—not only to one another, but also toward ourselves (Eph. 4:32).

Life is a series of peak-and-valley experiences. The good times don't last forever, but neither do the bad.

As long as we remember that one setback doesn't mean that we have lost everything, we can keep on keeping on. The struggles and the wear and tear are worth it when every so often, just when you need it most, your son gives you a quick hug and says, "You're the best mom in the world!"

Chapter
2

DISCIPLINE
It's a Dad's Job, Isn't It?

"You didn't say we couldn't have friends over while you were at work, just that we couldn't have friends in the house."

Jon knew what I had meant when I made the statement that when I was at work, no friends were allowed at the house. He had deliberately misinterpreted my instructions in order to do exactly what he wanted. Sound familiar? Okay, next time I was more explicit.

Often during those years of raising my sons alone, I found myself angry that I had to be the one to handle all of the discipline as well as all of the other aspects of being the head of a one-parent family. I had somehow grown up with the vague notion that the really tough discipline issues were a father's job! How often I had heard not only my own mother, but also my friends' mothers utter those dreaded words, "Wait until your father gets home!" Fathers were the ones who made the BIG decisions, who meted out justice, and who determined the exact consequences for childish "crimes."

Yet here I was at twenty-seven, a single mom having to do it all alone. And, in the area of discipline, I sometimes felt that I was playing a game where I didn't know the rules and wasn't very skillful. I read lots of books and tried every idea that seemed to make sense. Sometimes things worked well, at other times they didn't. At one particularly difficult period, I picked up a book written by some good friends of mine, Dave and Jan Stoop, entitled *The Total(ed) Parent* (Eugene, OR: Harvest House, 1978). Since Dave had a doctorate in psychology, I was sure the book would be helpful. It was, but not in the way I expected. I was looking for principles and steps to take, and what I found was another family, one with both a mother and a father, having similar problems to those I was having. How freeing to find that a man I admired was having difficulty being a parent. I decided that perhaps it would work the same for me—I could have problems, and still be okay!

The same is true for you too! If you feel uncomfortable at times as a disciplinarian, remember that you're not alone. Most parents wonder if what they are doing is right. In the area of teaching and training (disciplining) sons, there are no set methods. But here are some helpful hints:

1. *Children need to be given explicit, realistic rules for what is acceptable behavior in your family.* For best results, the rules should be discussed between the children and you before they are finalized and implemented. Why? The rules children help make are the ones they are most likely to keep. Also if there are concrete reasons for the rules (ones that the boys understand), the rules are less likely to be broken. Agree to

a set of related consequences for breaking the rules so children know what to expect if they choose not to follow the rules.

As my boys got older (about ten and twelve), we discussed house rules and possible consequences. Sometimes their suggestions for consequences were stricter than I was willing to enforce, but the discussions often resulted in their following the rules more willingly.

2. *Keep the rules realistic.* Do not make rules you will not or cannot enforce. Each time you do not enforce a rule, you further ruin your credibility with the children. Making rules which you have no way of monitoring or enforcing is useless.

You will want to watch out for power struggles when your sons become teenagers. Don't set rules just to prove that you are the parent without considering how you are going to enforce compliance. If you are 5'5", 110 lbs. and your son is 5'11", 180 lbs., how are you going to stop his going to a friend's house when you've told him he can't go? I tried to set consequences I could enforce. To my seventeen-year-old: "I'll pick you up outside the skating rink at 11:00 P.M. I will be there at 10:50 and wait until 11:10. If you aren't outside, you'll have to get a ride with a friend because I won't come back for you."

To my fifteen-year-old: "I will drive you to school if you are ready to leave at 7:30. But I have to leave right at 7:30 so I won't be late to work. If you are not ready, you'll have to walk and you'll be tardy."

Enforce the consequences. When you permit a rule to be broken without enforcing the consequences, you are giving a message that your son can break a rule and sometimes not have to pay the price.

3. Make sure the rules are age appropriate for your children. Don't be overprotective or so strict that you limit a child's natural creativity and spontaneity. Encourage responsible independence.

4. Expect the children to test the limits. Be prepared for manipulative testing of any limits you have agreed to as a family or have set as a parent. Instead of becoming angry, just recognize that this testing, this checking one's own limits and abilities, is a natural part of your son's growing up.

Isn't that how God deals with us? He has a set of rules that He has made for our own good, and He expects us to live according to those rules. When we fail to do so, we must take the consequences. We pay the price, we lose the joy of our fellowship with God, we feel bad, we experience less than successful living because of wrong choices. And yet knowing that, don't we sometimes act like children ourselves and test those limits? Don't we sometimes try to come as near to sinning as we can without crossing over the line? Of course we do. But when our sons do this, we become angry. Perhaps remembering that we are just as guilty as they are when it comes to breaking God's laws will make us more gentle in dealing with discipline problems. We do not need to lower our standards, but we may need to learn new ways to communicate and to discipline.

At some point you can expect your son's budding masculinity to exhibit itself as rebellion against your authority over him. It seems to be an unwritten rule that men are supposed to be the ones with the power and the authority. While daughters may compete with a mother for attention or position, sons tend more often to challenge a mother's right to authority. This happens not only to single moms but to any mother who disciplines her sons.

When choosing consequences for children's offenses, I am often mindful of Ephesians 6:4 which tells parents not to provoke their children to anger, but to bring them up in the nurture and admonition of the Lord. We can take lessons in discipline from God. He never changes His standards for us, but He is always willing to forgive, and He never stops loving us.

IF ONLY I HAD A DEGREE IN PARENTING

At work, Katherine is an effective executive in a major corporation. She deals with the daily challenges of managing a staff of 125 employees and supervisors with practiced ease. Her department consistently achieves its production goals, has the lowest absenteeism rate and the highest morale. Katherine firmly believes that a major factor in her success is that she has learned to involve her staff in the goal-setting and decision-making processes. "When people help set the goals," she explains, "they are more committed to doing the work to reach those goals." Because of her effectiveness, she will probably be made a vice president within the next several years.

At home, Katherine is also a manager. She plans the family budget and can squeeze more value out of a dollar than most of her friends. She organizes the schedule using time management principles so that, although everyone is extremely busy, all family members are ensured of having time for activities (soccer, music lessons, church choir), chores, homework, and play. She has divided the chores fairly among all family members according to age and ability. She developed house rules that all agree are reasonable and fair. Also she plans two hours a week of uninterrupted time to be alone with each of her three sons, ages seven, nine, and twelve. Although frequently exhausted, Katherine usually feels she is a good parent who does everything she can for her children. However, lately she has become frustrated because it seems the boys are determined to cause trouble. They are rebellious, uncooperative, disruptive, and demanding.

Sound familiar?

Katherine mused, "I went to college to learn how to be a good manager at work, and I have a degree in Business Administration. I was taught several approaches to management and the predictable outcomes of using each style. I have learned by experience which approaches work best for me in different situations, and those are the ones I use to be effective on the job. It works!" She laughs ruefully, "Maybe I should have gotten a degree in parenting!"

I am convinced that most of us mothers wish we had been more knowledgeable and skillful when we had our first child. But it is not too late to develop more effective ways of parenting if our current approach is not working. We can be successful parents if we put our minds to it and decide that we will do our very best.

REASONS BOYS MISBEHAVE

One of the ways that many of us evaluate ourselves as parents is based on how well-behaved our children are, how well they obey and how well they conform to the house rules. *A son's misbehavior is often interpreted to mean that we have not controlled him well enough.* Thus we often attempt to increase our authority, make more rules, and dish out more punishment/consequences. Frequently, we fail.

In such situations, it is more productive to recognize that "misbehavior" is a helpful clue that something is going on within the son to trigger those responses. Dr. Don Dinkmeyer and Dr. Gary McKay in their book *Systematic Training for Effective Parenting* suggest that there are four *goals* of misbehavior: attention, demonstrating inadequacy, revenge, and power. These goals are the result of some basic desires a boy may have.

1. To Get Attention

Seven-year-old Mike had a habit of interrupting me when I was reading, asking me to play a game with him. When I had friends over he tried to be the center of attention, bringing out toys to show the guests or clowning around. When I was on the telephone, he often started arguments with his brother or asked me questions.

The boy who wants excessive attention believes that he is only important when you are paying attention to him and serving him in some way. If he does not receive sufficient positive attention from you, he may choose to misbehave to gain at least some negative attention. Probably your response to his misbehaving is to feel annoyed, pestered, and irritated, which causes you to order, remind, nag, coax, or wheedle to get him to stop. These actions may result in his temporary cessation (since he received your attention), but he will start again when his need for attention again becomes important.

A more effective response might be to take notice of this pattern of misbehavior and recognize it as a signal that your son feels in need of attention. Find ways to give extra attention either before he misbehaves or as a reward for being quiet and not interrupting. Also, whenever possible, ignore his negative behaviors so that they are not reinforced by his receiving the desired attention. Once I figured this out, I used to try to give Mike extra attention before I started to read, make telephone calls, or have guests over. This met his needs and gave me the freedom to meet mine without his misbehavior.

2. To Demonstrate Inadequacy

Steve refuses to do his homework, repair his bike, work in the yard, or cook a meal. He'll do without before he will attempt something he considers difficult—and a lot of things look hard to him. Like Steve, some boys have such a sense of helplessness, a lack of self-confidence, that they feel they can't do anything. Rather than risking failure, they don't try; neither do they want us to expect them to.

Often their behaviors convince us that they are helpless and that it is hopeless to try to get them to do what we want. Therefore, we lower our expectations, make excuses for them, give up, and do the tasks ourselves. This, of course, only validates our children's feelings of inadequacy and they continue to fail and do incomplete work.

Wise mothers avoid criticism, don't give up, applaud progress (no matter how small), and encourage strengths and abilities. Sometimes when we allow our sons to struggle with a difficult chore, letting them know we think they can do it, they draw from our confidence to develop their own as they actually complete the task.

3. To Get Revenge

Geoff is a terror. He set fire to the new kitchen curtains and threw his mom's favorite vase into the fireplace, breaking it into a thousand pieces. He refuses to wear the new shirt his grandma sent and "forgets" to give his mom telephone messages.

A boy who feels unloved, for whatever real or imagined reason, tends to want to hurt others as much as he is hurting. Since we do love our sons, it is often hard for us to recognize such hateful behaviors as a sign of feeling unloved. Instead, since we feel hurt, unappreciated, and unloved ourselves, we cry, yell, punish, get even, or try to "teach them a lesson." However, these actions only trigger a vicious cycle when our sons respond by harboring resentment and looking for new opportunities to get even.

You can help your son with his need for a positive self-image and for security by working to build a relationship where he can trust you to accept him. Plan ways to communicate your acceptance on a daily basis. When you are both calm, discuss your feelings about the situations in which your son acts in hurtful ways.

4. To Exercise Power

"No matter what I tell him to do, Brad will do the opposite," complains Ruth, "from 'Eat your peas' to 'Wear your sweater'." Some boys have such a need for power that they constantly try to be in control, to prove that no one else is going to boss them around. When they behave in this way, we parents feel our authority being undermined, so we fight, overpower, bribe, threaten, or capitulate. In response, they may argue, have a tantrum, disobey, or submit angrily.

Many parents have found that they get better results by initially enlisting cooperation than by unilaterally setting rules (even if they are reasonable and fair). Remember Katherine, the good manager? She brought home most of her managerial skills, except the most important one: allowing participation in goal setting and decision making. When parents avoid setting up conflict situations, review options and consequences with their children (particularly those over six years old), and work cooperatively on making decisions, many of the children's power-seeking behaviors discontinue.

Some of the power struggles we get into with our children come from our trying to maintain control and protect our authority. We delude ourselves that we are the wise grownups whom God has put in charge, so we must know it all and be right. Parenting would be a lot easier if this were true. Although we acknowledge that statement to be false, we often act as if it were true, so we demand instant and unquestioning obedience simply "because I said so!"

HOW CAN I SUCCESSFULLY DISCIPLINE?

Disciplining is training your son to behave in a way consistent with your expectations or to take the consequences of his failure to live up to your standards. The discipline process centers around a series of conflicts over these standards.

Dr. Thomas Gordon, in his helpful book *Parent Effectiveness Training,* discusses in detail the three basic approaches to resolving parent-child conflicts. The same problem may be handled in these ways.

In *Method I* (a win-lose approach), the parent considers the various options and consequences, then chooses the best solution which he or she announces to the child, hoping it will be accepted. If it is not, the parent tries persuasion but will resort to power and authority to gain compliance if necessary. The parent is perceived to have *won* and the child to have *lost*.

In *Method II* (also a win-lose approach) the parent and child discuss the problem. Either the child doesn't accept the parent's solution or the child uses power to get the parent to go along with his own solution. The parent gives in and the child is said to have *won,* the parent to have *lost*.

There are several reasons why using power to resolve conflicts is undesirable, particularly as our sons reach adolescence. Enforcing our will may result in compliance but not in self-discipline or acceptance of our values. Power struggles take an inordinate amount of emotional, mental, psychological, and even physical energy. The loser will be angry and hostile toward the other. Furthermore, the parent will inevitably run out of power. When our sons are young, they depend upon us for everything, so it is easy to reward or punish to ensure compliance. But the older the boys get, the harder it is to find a "club" big enough to win a power struggle.

"As long as you live in my house, you won't do that!" yelled Becky at her sixteen-year-old, George.

"Fine," George responded. "I'll move out!" And he did.

"Just what do you say to a six-foot-tall, seventeen year old?" another mom, Lynne, asks. " 'Don't go out that door'? If he wants to, he will, and then what do you do?"

Because using power is not an effective approach, Dr. Gordon suggests *Method III* (a no-lose approach), in which both parties sit down and work toward a solution that is mutually acceptable. Although Dr. Gordon advocates using this method for children of any age, many parents are more comfortable using it with those who are older. Some parents initially find this approach totally unacceptable. However, we choose to use it with other adults when there is a conflict of needs because it works so well. Why not follow the same principle with our children, not only resolving disagreements, but also teaching an effective method to resolve other problems in the future?

An important goal I had for my sons was that they finish high school. Sixteen-year-old Jon had other ideas. He refused to attend class regularly and was unmoved by my tears, pleas, arguments, lectures, or demands. Finally, after a long power struggle, I admitted to myself that I was losing the battle and agreed to sit down and calmly discuss alternatives. He could go half days only to a special Basic Subjects School in lieu of going all day to regular high school (my choice). He could file for the California High School Proficiency Exam (his choice). There were several other options in between.

We finally reached a compromise agreement. He would take the test and if he passed, he would get a job. If he didn't, he'd go back to high school. He passed on the first try, which gave him the equivalent of a high school diploma. It wasn't what I wanted for him, but the result was the same: employability. He's held a steady job for the last several years as a computer programmer, is now married, and is doing well on his own.

SOMETIMES NOTHING I DO SEEMS RIGHT

In spite of everything, there will be times when you will end up in a deadlock. You and your son will be on opposite sides of an important issue and neither will be ready to give an inch, a frustrating and upsetting situation. You may have to make a really tough decision about where to go from there, a decision that may literally hurt you more than it does your son.

Rachael stood in the garage watching her son work on his car. In spite of numerous discussions about his reckless driving style, the impact of another accident on his insurance rates and driver's license, and his mother's many other reasons against it, he was planning to put a "souped-up" engine in his car. He was eighteen, had bought the engine with his own money, and was determined. Rachael determined she couldn't accept what she was sure would be the consequences of his having such a powerful engine in the car and quietly said, "If you put that engine in, I will no longer pay your insurance or carry you on my policy. Also, your things will be packed and moved out of my house tonight." She turned and went back into the house and held her breath. She knew he couldn't afford to move out on his own, but she wasn't sure he wouldn't do so anyway.

He didn't put the engine in. He also didn't speak to her for a week.

Six years later he thanked his mom for stopping him.

Mike was sixteen when he and a buddy were picked up by the police for breaking the law. His friend's parents went to the detention center and took their son home. However, because of several issues involved in the situation, I felt it best to have him experience the consequences of his actions. I let the authorities hold him until he could go before the judge. Each day I went to visit him, cried with him, and went home with his pleas and promises ringing in my ears. I was sure I was doing the wise thing, but it was so very hard. Each night I threw up, paced the floor, and wept. That was my "baby" locked up in juvenile hall. It was agony to see him hurting. At the hearing, the charges were dropped and I was free to take Mike home. I wasn't sure he would ever forgive me for leaving him in juvenile hall; but while there, Mike saw what jail/prison could be like and decided never again to get into trouble. And he never has since then.

How tough should we be? Only you can choose when you must be tough. But I've found that if I am tough when I'm angry, I may be wrong. However, if I hang tough when it is hard to, I'm possibly right.

How tender can we be? Very. Nothing is as strong as tenderness. Our children are precious. We need always to treat them gently with a lot of love.

Chapter

3

COMMUNICATION
Where Do I Learn Boy-Talk?

"Are you a boy?" the young Chavante brave demanded of me.

"Of course not! I am a girl!" I responded indignantly in Chavante.

"Well, you talk like a boy!" he retorted. "Girls are supposed to talk differently!"

I was fourteen and had spent the last several months living with my folks as missionaries to the Chavantes in the jungles of Brazil. I had made friends with several of the young boys in the tribe who were teaching me their language. (The young girls were too busy doing their daily chores to teach me.) It took a visiting brave to tell me that I had learned the wrong words! Sure enough, I had to start learning all over again, because in that tribe many words are different depending on the sex of the speaker!

There were times as a single mom that I felt as if I needed a crash course in boy-talk.

Sometimes as I listened to my sons and their friends

41

talking I wondered if I would ever learn to speak "boy-talk." At first, I tried to stay current with the slang, to know that "bad" meant "great" and "gross" meant "good." But I gave up on that! By the time I learned one set of words well enough to use them, the boys were using new phrases.

Next I tried to become proficient at discussing "boy topics" such as sports, bugs, and cars. But again, the things I studied on these subjects weren't of interest to the boys. So, I tried a new approach. I didn't pretend to be (or try to become) an expert on football, but I would watch the games with Mike. I didn't become a base-ball umpire, but I did go to every practice and Little League game and cheered for my sons' teams. I didn't learn all about cars, but when Jon said he wanted a Corvette, I agreed they were great cars and invited him to tell me what he liked most about them.

I found I didn't need to talk like a boy—if I listened like a caring friend. And when I quit trying so hard, I began to learn from my sons as I spent time paying attention and listening to them.

Interacting with my sons was simply a matter of practicing communication skills.

ESTABLISH AN OPEN CLIMATE

Angrily, but deliberately and quietly so we wouldn't be heard in the living room, I confronted my son in the kitchen. "Michael, you are embarrassing me in front of my friends." Each word was hissed through clenched teeth and accompanied by a practiced paren-tal glare.

"Stop yelling at me!" Michael screamed loudly.

Self-righteously, I snapped, "Michael, I am not yelling. I haven't even raised my voice!"

"It *feels* like you're yelling at me!" he countered.

And he was right. Except for the fact that I was nearly whispering, I *was* yelling at him. So often what our sons respond to is not so much the words we say, as the feeling they get from what we say or how we say it.

Conflicts between mothers and sons are daily occurrences in most households, partly because all too few of us have mastered good communication skills. We talk, but we don't always express ourselves clearly and appropriately. We hear, but we don't always listen. Communicating effectively is one of the big challenges we face as mothers raising sons alone.

Sometimes I have fantasized that children should come with "off-on" switches. Why is it that when I most want my teenager to share openly what he is thinking or feeling, he becomes stubbornly mute! And why, just when I am least able to cope with any additional stress, does he become eloquently vocal, saying things I wish he hadn't verbalized just then!

Sometimes the reason our sons clam up is that we tend to "punish" them for saying things we don't want to hear. I don't know how many times I had to almost bite my tongue to keep from responding with a sarcastic put-down to a comment from one of my sons. But with practice we can learn to hold back such nonproductive responses to create an open climate.

If we do not create an open climate for our children, they may not choose to share with us their deepest feelings and thoughts. It is true that sometimes when we encourage openness, we hear things we don't want to hear: criticism, longing for the other parent, resentment about living in a one-parent family, values that we don't share, and reminders about times when we have failed to be the best parent we could be. But, if we can learn to not "punish" children for sharing these things with us, we can speed up the time required for healing after a trauma such as divorce or losing a parent by death.

Sara came bouncing into my office one morning scarcely able to contain her excitement. "You won't believe what a good time my son and I had just talking last night," she exclaimed. "He came home in a lousy mood and we almost got into an argument over something he said. Then I decided that maybe we could talk about his day and he really opened up. I'm glad I didn't yell at him for being upset, because he had a good reason to be! Anyway, after he started sharing, we just talked and talked for hours, about all kinds of things. It felt great!"

It is exciting to communicate well with our sons. If this has been a problem, encourage openness in these ways:

1. Be open yourself.
2. Learn to phrase discussion-starting questions by avoiding those that can be answered with a simple "yes" or "no."
3. Practice good listening skills.
4. Respond honestly, but kindly. It is all right to describe how you feel about what the children say, as long as you acknowledge their right to share openly.

If we fail to provide an open climate, our children might eventually stop sharing altogether. We need to be willing to discuss any subject or problem with our sons. We may not have all of the answers, but we can search them out together. If we cut off some subjects as taboo, we are closing areas of communication. This is not to say that we don't reserve the right to choose the time for some discussions that may be painful, embarrassing, or difficult. Each of us must decide when our personal privacy requires some reticence. An example might be our opinion of an ex-spouse or someone else whom our sons value highly, and we don't.

Timing is important. We had a rule at our house. I would discuss anything with the boys, but not when any of us were angry. I don't communicate well when I am angry, and neither do they. It was comical one day when Jon was anxious to discuss his need for money after he had overspent his allowance—again. He kept coming back to me about every ten minutes asking if I was calmed down yet. Finally, I could say yes and we worked things out.

HANDLE THE QUESTIONS

Sometimes children will ask hard-to-answer questions or the same questions over and over again. When Ted and Cathy were divorced they gave a simple but honest explanation to the children. Yet each year after visiting their father during the summer, the children would come back and query Cathy, "Why were you and Dad really divorced?" It was as if now that another year had passed, they might be given the *real* story. It seemed that they were looking for another reason than that which had been given them. Finally Cathy came to understand that there was a question behind the questions that needed answering. This is usually the case when children ask the same question many times.

I had the same experience. Each year after the boys returned from visiting their father, they wanted to talk about why we had been divorced. I don't know if he got the same questions, but I grew tired of always trying to explain something I didn't even understand myself. However, once I understood what was behind the questions, I was able to handle them better.

Here are some unspoken questions that single moms need to be sensitive to.

1. Was I responsible?

Experts agree that most children feel that in some way they were responsible for the breakup of the marriage. If only they had been more obedient, quiet, studious, cheerful, helpful, or independent, the marriage would have lasted, they reason.

Five-year-old Jimmy had never had a father-in-residence because his father disappeared before he was born, yet one day he asked his mom if she and his dad had ever been happy together. When she said that they had been happy when they first got together, he started to cry. "Then I guess it was because of me that he left, huh?" Jimmy sobbed.

You may need to reassure your sons that they were not responsible for a decision to end a marriage relationship, and this may have to be repeated more than once. It takes time to change a belief.

2. Will you ever leave me?

It is understandable that young boys who have lost

a parent by death or divorce will fear that the second parent may also leave. Being extra accountable for your whereabouts and expected time of return can help alleviate this fear. Whenever possible, let them know how to reach you by telephone. Call home if you are going to be gone long or will return later than expected.

3. Will I always be loved?

This is a question many adults would like answered. To a child who had just learned that romantic love between a husband and a wife doesn't always last forever, the possibility of parental love not lasting can be frightening. Remember to say frequently, "I love you." Affirm your love by what you do for your children. Only time will truly convince the children that they are truly loved.

Many of the unasked questions stem from these three fears that children have, but there may be others. Listen carefully to your children's questions to hear what they wish they could ask, and try to answer both questions. Encourage them to express feelings as well as to ask questions and attempt to set an open climate for both.

Even as an adult I used to have some of the same questions myself. Whenever I began a new relationship with a man, I found myself wondering if he would always care for me; if he, too, would leave me; and if anything that went wrong with the relationship were my fault. Understanding my own insecurities helped me deal with those of the boys. I made sure that each day I asked God for guidance in how best to demonstrate love and to reassure the boys that they were safe and loved.

If we want our sons to be open with us, then we as parents must sensitively find ways to create an open atmosphere in which our children will share. Timing is important. A wise parent will know not to bring up major conflict issues when there is insufficient time for a full discussion, or when one or both parties are tired, hungry, or upset. Observant moms notice which of their sons can handle direct confrontations and which need a softer approach. Trying to force children to communicate in the way we want rather than their way only causes additional and unnecessary stress.

Elaine liked to sit down face-to-face with another person to work through a conflict or difficult issue. She found, however, that this approach was not comfortable for her son who reacted by clamming up, leaving her frustrated and angry. One day, driving to the grocery store with her son, she brought up the subject of his poor grade in history. Glenn chatted freely about the difficulty he was having and how he felt about the type of homework assignments he was given. They came up with an approach to studying that eventually raised his grade. Elaine realized that Glenn talked more freely when they were also doing other things such as washing dishes, preparing dinner, or working in the garden. Soon she learned to reserve difficult topics for discussion during those times when Glenn would be comfortable considering them. She had discovered the secret of getting him to open up.

WATCH HOW YOU PHRASE
WHAT YOU SAY

Glenn confided to Elaine during one of their talks in the car that he felt that he was always disappointing her and that she was unhappy with him. Elaine then scrutinized the ways she shared her feelings with Glenn. Most of us could stand a second look at ourselves in this area. Often when we most want cooperation from our sons, we instead trigger angry or resentful feelings by what we say to them. We could heed what Paul says to Timothy in 1 Timothy 4:12: "Be an example to the believers, in word, in conduct, in love, in spirit, in purity." That may be hard to do sometimes, but it's necessary.

Adele Faber and Elaine Mazlish, authors of *How to Talk So Kids Will Listen and Listen So Kids Will Talk,* have a list of unhelpful statements we often make: We blame ("You broke it, now fix it!"). We call names ("How could you be so stupid?"). We lecture ("I've told you a hundred times before . . ."). We deny ("You can't be thirsty, you just had a soda!").

One solution is to use empathetic statements. Acknowledging children's feelings does not necessarily mean that we condone them. It merely signifies that we recognize them.

When Tommy stubbornly refuses to go to bed on time and starts crying angrily, Mother says, "Seems like you really want to stay up so you can play longer. You are very upset about having to go to bed right now." When Tommy responds by sharing his angry feelings, he learns that it is acceptable to express feelings and be understood, but it is still bedtime. The parent is still in charge, and the child is free to express his feelings.

The next time your son confronts you with an angry or hateful statement, try acknowledging the feeling behind what he is saying.

To "I hate you," say, "It sounds as if you are very upset with me over this."

To "You never listen to my side," say, "You must feel ignored. I will listen now."

To "You never do anything I ask you to do!" say, "It sounds as if you don't feel that I really care about your wishes. Tell me more about that."

Sometimes it is hard not to get pulled into an argument, but the more you practice using the new responses, the easier they become. There are other words to watch for and avoid. Don't belittle your son, no matter how angry you are. Never apply negative labels, which tend to stick in the minds of children and may become self-fulfilling prophecies. Therefore don't call your son a "slow learner," "lazy," "a pessimist," a "liar," or a "scatterbrain."

As you develop special awareness to the way you express yourself in conversations with your sons, you may find areas that need corrective attention. If so, set realistic goals and start practicing the skills you want to master. Soon you will be very good at using them.

Expressing Your Feelings Honestly, But Appropriately

Eleven-year-old Carl gave his mother a hug on his way out of the door for school, saying, "I love you, Mom." Fran felt warm, loved, and satisfied—until she walked past the open door to Carl's room. It was a mess: dirty dishes from midnight snacks on the dresser and under the bed, clothes strewn everywhere. Remembering Carl's promise the night before to clean his room, Fran felt her anger rise and the good feelings disappear. All day she stewed, waiting for him to get home, then she attacked.

"You make me so mad!" she began, and the fight was on.

Sometimes we want to express how we feel to our children. At times we may be understandably angry, hurt, disappointed, or let down. We *can* share these feelings in an appropriate manner. The first rule is to use an "I" message. Start a sentence with "I feel . . ." rather than "You make me feel . . ." This carries the point in a nonthreatening manner.

It would have been better had Fran waited until Carl came into the kitchen for a snack. Then she could have said, "I feel let down and disappointed. When you make promises you don't keep, I feel that you don't love me. So when I saw your room was still a mess, I was angry, sad, and hurt."

There's no guarantee that Carl's response would have been a contrite "I'm sorry" and a move to clean his room immediately, but most likely his response would have been better to an "I" message than to a "You" accusation.

A second rule is to state a request clearly. "Please wipe your feet before you step on the clean floor" is much better than "If you had any sense you would have seen that my floor is clean and not walked in with muddy feet!"

We can even express strong anger, as long as we stop short of saying damaging things about our sons. If the living room is strewn with toys after the boys were told not to make a mess, we might say firmly (and even loudly), "I am upset! I don't like being ignored! Company will be here in twenty minutes and there are toys everywhere!" It isn't necessary to add "you little slobs!"

A third rule is not to hide the real message in rhetoric. Instead of saying, "Some kids love their parents enough to let them know if they are going to be late from school," be more direct and say, "Please call me if you are going to be late coming home from school."

Lectures Are Usually Wasted!

Kids get awfully tired of our lectures. Most parents have a long list of lectures we deliver at appropriate moments. Maybe we could just number them and call out the number when we feel a lecture is needed. The children would probably appreciate it! Lecturing is talking *to* the boys instead of talking *with* them. *Talking to* builds resentment. *Talking with* builds relationships.

If you find yourself frequently lecturing or nagging, you may wish to choose different ways of handling these situations. I had a standard list of rules I would reiterate whenever the boys wanted to have overnight guests. "Yes, if you'll go to bed on time, if you won't fight, if you'll include your brother, if you won't eat in the bedroom . . ."

One day I noticed that Jon was nodding his head impatiently as I rattled off the list. I had a brainstorm. I stopped and said, "You know the rules. You tell me!" And he did, word perfectly! From then on I used that technique with the boys. Whenever I was tempted to nag or lecture, I would ask:

"What are the rules about going to visit your friends after school?"

"What were you supposed to do this morning?"

"What do you have to do before you participate in another club or on a team?"

It worked very well! Try it!

LEARN TO LISTEN CAREFULLY

Sometimes a person who is very good at expressing thoughts and ideas is not very good at listening to others, particularly to those who have difficulty expressing themselves well. Attentive listening communicates a lot to the speaker. It conveys interest, respect, and caring. It says, "I value you and think you have something to contribute."

If we are truly listening to another, we are focusing on what is being said rather than interrupting, judging, reacting to what is being said, or planning what we want to say in response. When we glance around, drum our fingers, appear impatient or sigh, we are telling the speaker we wish he/she would shut up. We may need to practice good listening behaviors in order to improve our listening skills.

A few years ago my son came into the kitchen after school. "I'm really angry," he said. "I think my teacher is wrong. She wrote on my referral slip that I did not try to do the work in class. I do so try. I am mad—very mad!" Although expressive, he didn't raise his voice.

I was so busy preparing supper that I merely nodded, making a comment here and there as he poured out the whole story. That night just as I was climbing into bed, it hit me! My son, the one who had never expressed anger verbally, who was better known to smash a wall, or clam up and seethe inside, had finally made a breakthrough—and I had almost missed it! I wanted to run, wake him, and shout for joy. But I waited.

The next morning at breakfast I complimented the way he had put his feelings into words. I radiated parental pride.

"I know. Guess I'm growing up, huh?" he responded offhandedly, as if growing up were an everyday occurrence. "Do we have any jelly for the toast?"

The good news is that they do grow up. The question is, will we have taught them good communication skills and maintained an open relationship with them along the way? True, good communication takes a lot of work and sometimes we end up hearing things we wish they hadn't said. But if we think the cost of encouraging our sons to be open is too high, we mustn't forget the cost of not allowing openness. The first might cost only some hurt feelings; the second could cost us our sons, if they clam up and refuse to communicate with us at all.

Let's speak the truth in love and listen with understanding and empathy.

ASK FORGIVENESS WHEN NECESSARY

You may find it hard to ask your sons' forgiveness when you have failed to communicate lovingly and honestly with them. But it is a necessary act. It reopens the channels of communication, and it allows you to practice what you preach. How can you teach your sons to be caring and forgiving, as God wants them to be, if you don't set a good example? Ephesians 4:32 says for us to be kind one to another, tender-hearted and forgiving one another, just as God for Christ's sake has forgiven us. That may be a tough standard to live up to, but that is the goal.

Just remember that you are serving as a role model, so become more accountable for what you say.

Chapter

4

FEMALE RELATIONSHIPS
What About the Women in His Life?

Over the years the boys and I have had our ups and downs, our times of conflict and of closeness. But nothing warms my heart more than to have one of them say sincerely, "I love you, Mom. I miss you terribly."

There's a special relationship that develops between mothers and sons, which is intensified when the mom is raising the sons alone. This relationship will be the single most important one in his life during the early years, sometimes for always.

Only mothers are privy to a series of intimacies that over the years forge strong bonds at a subliminal level. Sons allow mothers to nurture, hug, kiss, nurse, bind up wounds, and see them cry, although allowing any other person to do so would be embarrassing and intolerable.

A son sometimes enjoys being protected by his mother as she instinctively rushes to his defense or rescue when he is criticized, attacked, or threatened. This lioness-protecting-her-cubs situation is not seen as threatening to his male ego in the early years and leaves the boy with a warm feeling of being valued.

In turn, as a boy grows into adolescence, he usually develops a sense of protectiveness toward his mother. A daughter, on the other hand, can develop a competitive spirit toward her mother, often resenting any love and attention the mother receives.

Finally, a boy learns how to relate to women in general from his relationship with his mother. All of this goes into making a mother's relationship with her son of supreme importance in his life.

Beth laid aside another of her many books on parenting and sighed. "Sometimes I feel so frightened that I will do something wrong and mess up my son's life forever!" she confessed.

Perfect parenting is a myth, but most parents try to come as close as they can to doing the right thing, saying the right words, and making the right choices. The problem is that there is not always one right choice to make. Here are some hints from other single moms.

YOU CAN EXPECT RESPECT

"I expect respect from my sons," Wilma explained, "even when I don't feel as if I really deserve it. The boys know that I will encourage them to express their feelings, their ideas and demands, but they must do so with respect for my position as their mother."

Boys who learn to respect (to not fear or be intimidated by) you as the head of the family will later be more likely to respect other women, their wives, and people in authority in the community and in their careers. "If you as a mother are ever tempted to let your son get by with talking to you in ways that are disrespectful just to avoid making a fuss, ask yourself if you would like to see him talk that way to his wife when he is married," Wilma said. "That ought to make you want to teach him to respect others!"

Wilma continued, "I feel it is very important that I am respectful also. Not only do I model respect for those in authority, but I also try to treat the boys in a way that maintains their dignity. I respect their privacy by knocking before entering their rooms, by not reading their mail, or listening in on their telephone conversations. I respect their dignity by not putting them down, calling them names, or making fun of them with my friends."

In order to warrant respect, you need to be respectful of others. During your family devotions, you might wish to have a scripture search on what God says about respecting one's parents. Use verses such as Ephesians 6:1–2; Colossians 3:20; Exodus 20:12; Deuteronomy 5:16; Matthew 15:4; Matthew 19:19; Mark 7:10. Also be sure to include verses about your responsibilities toward your sons and in the parenting role so that the discussion doesn't turn into a sermon instead of an exploration of what God has in mind for you in your different roles as mothers and sons.

ALLOW HIM HIS CHILDHOOD

"I work hard at balancing my expectations of my son, Jeff," Sherry explained, "because I believe that he is entitled to his childhood. If he doesn't get one now, he may take it later when he is forty plus. Better now than then."

I think Sherry has a valid point. Chad's mother was widowed when he was ten. Immediately, his paper route income became necessary for the family's survival. His mom went to work, so Chad helped with the housework and took over much of the care of his two younger sisters. After school he supervised their homework, kept them entertained, cooked dinner, and helped clean up afterwards. He grew up to be a self-sufficient, well-behaved, and responsible young man. He married, had three kids, worked at a boring but comfortably paying job, and did well for several years. Suddenly one day, without any warning, he left his wife, quit his job, and went to Aspen to ski all winter. Later, he described his experience. "I felt that life had passed me by, that all I'd known was hard work and responsibility. I wanted to play like everyone else. I had to get out from under everything, even if I lost it all—which I did!"

What a price to pay for a delayed childhood!

It is important that you not look to a son to be the "man of the house." A boy is not ready to take on the spousal roles of provider or protector, although he can be of tremendous assistance in these areas, particularly with younger brothers and sisters. Increase his responsibilities and duties, but reserve the role of head of the house for yourself. It requires an adult; and when there's only one parent, there's no choice—it is you.

ENCOURAGE THE TENDER SIDE

"Be sure to affirm [encourage] the tender qualities in your son," suggested Jody, a social worker who works with kids in a juvenile hall. "So many of the boys I see on my job are crying out for love, but they don't know how to ask for or receive a hug."

Each of us has a tough and a tender side. The tough guy image is often reinforced in our sons by us, by society, and by peers. But tenderness, sensitivity, kindness, and gentleness are also qualities we will want to affirm in our sons. A person who can acknowledge both sides of his personality is stronger and more ready to face the struggles of living in the world today. So, we must not be guilty of using the old cliché, "Boys don't cry." If our son is hurt, tears may be very appropriate. Let him be the whole person he was created to be.

A good way to provide an outlet for expressing love, for touching and caring for another, is to allow children to have pets. It is socially acceptable for a boy to love his pets, to romp and cuddle with them.

Some of my favorite men friends are those who cry with me at the movies, who love to cuddle newborn puppies, and who catch their breath at a gorgeous sunset. I appreciate the tender side of the men in my life.

Take a look at Galatians 5:22–23 where nine manifestations of the fruit of the Spirit are listed. At least five of these reflect the tender side of our personalities. These characteristics of the Holy Spirit are present in our lives as believers if we allow Him to mold our character: peace, patience, gentleness, goodness, and meekness. We need to affirm those characteristics in our sons not only as desirable, but as ways they can manifest the work of the Holy Spirit in their lives. There are many verses that urge us to be kind, tenderhearted, gentle, and to love one another. Developing these characteristics does not diminish the masculinity of a young man.

LET HIM KNOW YOU'RE HUMAN

One day when my son was about twelve, he came into the living room when I was visiting and laughing uproariously with my friends. I turned around and saw him looking at me in astonishment. When I asked him what was the matter, he said he had never seen me act silly before! Right then I realized that I had tried so hard to be strong and responsible that I had rarely let down my guard and never in front of my son.

What about you? Can your son really describe you? Does he know what you dream of, what you like, what you fear, what makes you cry? Can he tell a joke that causes you to laugh? In other words, does your son know the real you, or just the you in the role of Mother? One reason to relate to your son not only as a parent but also as a person is that your parenting role will terminate within a few years. Then your adult relationship should be one between two grownups, not between parent and child.

On the other hand, do you know your son as a person, or just in his role as your child? Perhaps you need to spend some time getting acquainted with one another. You may be surprised at what good friends you can become.

IF YOU ARE A WEEKEND PARENT

Some mothers do not have custody of their sons during the week but only on weekends. These mothers have a special challenge. If you are struggling to adjust to this situation, perhaps these ideas will help.

Recognize the Positives

Weekends provide large blocks of time together that are great for taking trips, going camping, visiting friends and family, working on joint projects, or attending special events. You don't have to go to work and they don't have to go to school. Your time is usually more casual and relaxed, allowing you both to have an opportunity to communicate and relate better than you might have during a busy work or school week.

Acknowledge the Negatives

Having your sons on weekends can have a negative side, however. Sometimes one or both of you are so tired from the week that all you want to do is sleep in late and laze around the house. You may not feel like being "up" for one another. Children who are active in the church youth group, team sports, or community groups may have scheduled events on weekends so they are not free to be together with you or fit in with your plans. As children grow older, they don't always want to spend time with their parents on weekends but prefer to make plans with their own friends. Of course, having the boys every weekend can also limit your own social life.

Plan for Success

As many once-a-week parents have discovered, weekend parenting is neither positive or negative automatically. It is what you make of it, so plan for success!

1. Plan a Realistic Schedule

Take a close look at your needs and the needs of the children and the other parent. Make a schedule, taking into account all of these. But keep the schedule flexible because there will be times when you may need to make alternative arrangements. At other times, you will need to allow the children's needs to take precedence over your own wishes. If you are willing to give a little, the others are more likely to be willing to do so.

2. Include a Variety of Activities

Plan a variety of chores, fun things, trips, and events, yet always allow for free time so you can relax and be spontaneous. Encourage the children to learn to entertain themselves. As much as you can, involve them in planning the events of the weekend. This can teach them to make wise choices and decisions. Don't be afraid to try a few new things the children suggest. You might learn something yourself!

One of the advantages of having your sons on a weekend is that you have an opportunity to include them in your spiritual activities, such as going to church and Sunday school together, and to instill in them Christian values. Even if they have a Christian father, it is good to be able to share your faith with those closest to you. No matter how tempted you are to maximize the amount of time you have together by giving up going to church, don't do that. Perhaps you could achieve the same results by getting up in time to go to the early service, but don't give up sharing your spiritual life together. Besides, Hebrews 10:25 tells us not to forsake the assembling of ourselves together. We need the fellowship of the believers to keep us strong and the Word of God (not only on Sundays) to equip us to fight the daily fight (Eph. 6:10–18).

Not every weekend will be an unqualified success, but each weekend can be a profitable experience for you and your children. Tough times can help you model how you've learned to cope when things are less than what you would want them to be. So make your weekends successful. The choice is yours.

WHEN HE STARTS TO DATE

"Don't push your son into dating," Lucy recommended. "I think I tried to at first. I kept asking if he was going to this or that party and if he was going to take a girl. Finally I realized that Larry would start dating when he was ready and not before. I butted out."

Many moms seem to be grouped at the two ends of the continuum. Some are so anxious for their sons to grow up, they welcome dating as a sign of budding maturity. Others view dating as a reminder that they will soon be losing their sons to independence, so try to delay the passing of time. There is no set age when boys are ready to go out with girls because each boy develops at his own rate.

At first "dating" will probably mean going to school parties, studying together, and doing group activities such as roller skating and bowling. However, at some point in the process of growing up, your son will single out one special girl and fall in love. This is the time when you will begin to see how his future relationships with women will be. Is he selfish, always demanding his own way? Is he timid, always going along with what she wants? Does he overspend on dates to impress her? With these clues, you should consider providing feedback to him. Choose a time when you will not be interrupted and calmly share how you as a woman would respond to a man who does what your son is doing. Dee does this. "I tell my son that while I was never a young man, I was a young girl, and I know how girls feel and think. When I explain that I am not trying to tell him what to do, just what the response might be to his actions, my son tends to listen," she says.

Sometimes jealousy is a real problem. Suddenly we see our boys behaving like men, being helpful, courteous, responsible toward another woman, and we wish they treated us that way. Here we need to deal with our jealousy honestly, recognizing that if they are relating well, it is a good sign that we have done something right. Be happy about that. We want our sons to grow up with the ability to have good relationships with the opposite sex. We want them to be assertive yet considerate, thrifty yet generous.

Be prepared to have your role in your son's life change when your son marries. At first you may feel excluded as another woman develops an intimate relationship with your son. Give them time to work out their new relationship. No one will ever take your place in his life, for you are his mother.

WHAT ABOUT A STEPMOTHER?

"I can handle the fact that my sixteen year old dates and has a great relationship with the mother of one of his friends, but what is really hard is that he gets along so well with his stepmother. I'm always hearing how wonderful she is. I hate it!" Shelly admits.

There can be a basic resentment on the part of a mother toward her son's stepmother. Perhaps there is a sense of territorialism about the ex-husband and the sons. Maybe there is a little envy that another woman is having a happy relationship with the former husband. Fear is typical. What if our children go to visit and like the stepparent more than they like us? We may become hostile to the stepmother or attempt to compete and become superparent trying to win our sons' undying admiration and love. Neither approach is productive.

Protectiveness is another response. If we think that the stepmother is less than tolerant, loving, generous, or kind to our sons, we tend to bring out the big guns, ready to do battle. Nevertheless, hard as it is to accept, we can't fight our children's battles for them.

On the other hand, some stepmothers have values and standards that are closer to those of the children than the ones we hold dear. The children see the stepmother as more permissive and fun to be with. But we see her as potentially harmful to our sons.

Maybe your response is gratitude. Now there is another adult to help with the responsibility of raising and supervising your sons. Maybe the stepmother is able to be patient in one area you can't be, or to motivate them to new achievements, or get them to listen to something you've been saying for years. Instead of being envious, you have learned to be grateful. If so, that is terrific!

In reality, many stepmothers are in a good position to have excellent relationships with their stepchildren. The stepmother may only see the children on the occasional weekend, and therefore the visits tend to be fun and exciting. Children don't often realize that if they lived at the other home, the day-to-day realities would be much different from the infrequent visits. If the stepmother doesn't have a career outside of the home, she may be free to do the extra things with the children that are difficult for a working mother to fit in. Finally, because some people are better at parenting than others, there are some stepmothers who make real mothers feel inadequate.

If there is a problem, the ideal solution is to recognize the fears you have about your son's relationship with his stepmother and see if you are the one creating the friction. Perhaps you could arrange to meet with the stepmother and calmly discuss any legitimate concerns you have. At the very least, you will want to remember that you are capable of loving more than one person at a time and so are your sons. Try to look at the stepmother as one more adult who is trying to help with the rearing of your son rather than as a competitor.

There will always be other women in your son's life, but his one-and-only mom has a special relationship. Work to make that relationship the best it can be.

Chapter
5

MALE RELATIONSHIPS
We Both Need Them!

"I get to see Dad this weekend," seven-year-old Randy announced, excitement evident in his voice, face, and even in the way he jumped up and down. Gail, his mother, watched with mixed emotions. Later, when Randy had gone outside to play, she voiced her thoughts.

"I know he needs contact with his dad, but there's a part of me who's scared he might turn out to be like his father, and that would kill me!"

Gail was raising her son alone, not because she was divorced, widowed, or unwed, but because her husband was in prison for armed robbery. She had legitimate fears about her son's father as a role model, yet she knew how important it is for a boy to have good rapport with the men in his life.

Sandy, an unwed mother of a six year old, confided, "I'd like for my son, Alex, to have a relationship with his father, but we don't know where he is. I do what I can to provide surrogate father figures for Alex."

Mary confessed: "It's not just my son who is looking for male companionship. I could use some!"

Both you and your son need healthy relationships with men, so do what you can to develop and encourage them. It may be a challenge to find the right men, but you can do it.

DAD IS IMPORTANT, SO ENCOURAGE THAT RELATIONSHIP

Many single moms fear that continued association with the dads will be harmful for their sons; but whenever possible, boys need that contact.

A dad is important in a boy's life for many reasons. Initially, a boy's self-concept comes from both parents. He needs a male role model. The relationship between a boy and his father provides the foundation for future relationships with other men. Also, a boy needs to be loved by both his mother and his dad. While surrogate fathers can provide for most of these needs if real fathers are not available, they are, at best, substitutes. Therefore, in most cases, moms should encourage the sons and their fathers to spend time together whenever possible. The mother should reinforce the relationship even if physical contact is minimal because of geographical distance.

This was the case with my sons, so I worked hard to encourage a good relationship between the boys and their father. We sent copies to their dad of school photos, grade cards, and any special achievement notices. I gave the boys photos of their dad to hang in their room. (The photos can be out-of-sight from the doorway, if seeing them is painful for the mother.)

We remembered to include their dad in our evening prayers. I carefully refrained from making derogatory remarks about my former husband in the presence of the boys.

I affirmed attributes in my sons that were like their father, including physical characteristics and preferences in movies, food, or activities. One day I noticed that Mike was thoroughly enjoying a second helping of dessert. On impulse, I said, "Mike, that was your father's favorite dessert!" He looked up, a big smile covering his face as he sat taller in his chair, and reached for a third helping.

Just telling your son that it is okay to love his dad isn't enough. You must give him proof by doing things which demonstrate that you mean it. You'll be giving your son a gift beyond price.

If a father is abusive or his home is unsafe for the boy, then visits may need to be short or in a neutral location, supervised if possible. Sue insisted that her ex-husband see the boys at his mother's house and only when his mother was there. You might arrange for your sons to meet or visit their dad only in public places such as skating rinks or bowling alleys, if such restrictions are necessary. You may need to limit the length of visits if prolonged contact tends to increase the tension between the boys and their father to the point of causing potential problems.

However, in many cases, our fears are exaggerated. Jan's former husband was a terrible spendthrift, always living just one step ahead of his creditors. She worried that their son, Joel, would adopt that lifestyle. At first, after visiting his father, Joel would complain about her lack of a microwave oven, a video cassette recorder, or a remote-controlled television. Jan's explanations of "we can't afford one" were met with assertions that Dad could! Jan was sure that her fears were being realized until a few years later Joel told his Mom, "I don't understand Dad. He's always in debt and he even writes checks when he doesn't have money in the bank!" She knew then that Joel was going to be okay.

Hazel's concern was that fourteen-year-old Paul would want to copy his father's lifestyle by having several romantic relationships at the same time. But after a year of visiting his dad almost every weekend, Paul told a friend, "Dad seems afraid of close relationships with women. I feel sort of sorry for him because I don't think he'll ever be happy." Overhearing this remark, Hazel relaxed.

Of course, there is always a possibility that a son will adopt values and a lifestyle that are contrary to the mother's. However, he could pick them up from a variety of other sources, even if he were isolated from a father believed to be a bad example. Therefore any decision to restrict or limit the relationship a boy has with his father should be very carefully considered. Mothers who have done so have this to share:

Patti: "I've become the 'bad guy' in Gary's mind since I got a court order to restrict his father's visits. Even though I had to do it, I'm sometimes tempted to give in. It is hard to feel your son hates you."

Kate: "I've found that my son sort of idealizes his dad because he has almost no contact with him. Dad is larger than life and a great fantasy. My son wants to be just like his dad."

Molly: "Chip has rejected his father, even more since

I limited his visits. His self-esteem seems to be lower than ever because he is identifying with having a 'bad dad'. I'm not sure what to do."

These experiences are not unique. The family, as it was originally designed, included both a mother and a dad. Ideally, this combination would provide the best possible setting in which a child could grow up and mature into a whole human being. In this ideal family, the mother would serve as a good role model for the daughters, the father for the sons. Here the sons would learn to relate to women as their relationship with their sisters and mothers developed; and daughters would learn to relate to men as they related to brothers and their father. The children would learn to share and to communicate well with adults and children, men and women, because of their family relationships. In this ideal family the children would be brought up with sound spiritual guidance and would develop positive self-images under discipline and affirmation from their parents. They would learn the principles of a loving man-woman relationship by observing their parents' marriage. The emotional, task, and responsibility workload of parenting would be shared equally by Mom and Dad.

Most single parent families fall very short of that ideal, but so do many two parent families! So don't become depressed and discouraged because your son doesn't have two parents in the home. Just be thankful that he has you to care for him, love him, and provide for his needs.

SONS ARE NOT PRIZES
OR POSSESSIONS

Some mothers forget that their sons are human beings and think of them as possessions instead. Having custody of the boys is seen as public recognition for being the better parent. But children are not prizes awarded by the court. Often custody is awarded to the mother because of tradition rather than because she is better for the children. Thus, instead of considering custody a reward, mothers need to consider it a precious responsibility.

Being a spouse and a parent are two different roles that require different skills. Just because a person never learned to be a good partner in a marriage relationship doesn't mean that he/she can't be a good parent. Often a man who wasn't close to his sons during the marriage and wasn't perceived as a good parent, becomes a fine parent after a divorce. People should not be judged entirely on their prior performance.

The fact that two people have not learned how to relate to one another within the intimacy of a marriage relationship, or that one person hasn't demonstrated good parenting skills, is no reason to absolve him (or her) of the responsibility to develop in the parental area. As stewards of the children God has entrusted to them, both parents are required to be faithful in fulfilling the trust. 1 Corinthians 4:2 says that "it is required in stewards that one be found faithful."

Later in that same passage, Paul reminds us that we don't know everything and that only the Lord knows what is in the heart of a person or in the future.

We mustn't pride ourselves on being better than anyone else, because if we are anything good, it is by the power of God. If God can help us become good parents, then He can do the same for someone else.

Another point to keep in mind is that throughout scripture where children are told to respect, obey, and honor their parents, both are listed, not just one. They are not told to honor the better one or the one who is perfect or the one who is good, kind, wise, or loving. Both parents are important in a child's life. And both parents can fail. In Romans 7:15–25, Paul talks about the inner struggle to be perfect. He acknowledges that at times he does what he doesn't want to and sometimes can't do what he wants to do and knows is right.

I often found myself identifying with Paul when I found that I just wasn't as "perfect" as I truly wanted to be as a parent.

MINIMIZE CONFLICTS WITH A HOSTILE EX-SPOUSE

Even though one of the best gifts you can give your son is the freedom to develop a warm, loving relationship with his other parent, you might be worrying about hostility from his dad. Not infrequently one parent is ready to develop a cooperative relationship while the other parent chooses to play destructive games. It is helpful in those situations to look beyond the negative behaviors and to recognize that they are usually triggered by severe, personal pain, which the individuals have not yet found positive ways to resolve. You can help your son by understanding and forgiving your spouse instead of playing games yourself.

If all of your efforts to develop a cooperative relationship with your former spouse have failed, minimize the conflicts as much as you can. Here are some examples.

1. If telephone conversations between the two of you always end in arguments, communicate in person, write letters, or have the boys telephone to make their own arrangements with their dad.

2. If pick-up and drop-off times trigger a confrontation between the two of you, defuse the situation by having a friend or relative present during those times. Be sure it is someone the boys' father respects and not someone whose presence would trigger another unpleasant incident. As another option, plan for the exchange to occur in a mutually acceptable location such as a sitter's or a relative's home where you need not be present. Also, you could simply refuse to discuss problems at those times.

3. If your former spouse always seems to call at inconvenient times and this frustrates you, such as at dinner time, when you have friends over, or late at night, courteously ask for the call to be returned at a later time, agree on a specific time when calls will be made to one another, unplug the phone when you don't want calls, or purchase an answering machine.

4. If the problem is that you are never sure if the boy's dad is going to follow through with his plans to do things with him, make contingency plans. Why waste your energies being anxious and frustrated?

By taking a positive approach, you will not only be improving the situation but also will be teaching your children a valuable lesson in accepting and relating to people.

"I had to take a good look at myself," Trisha confessed, "and I found that I was causing part of the problems between me and my ex-husband, and the boys were taking the brunt of our anger."

Sometimes the problem *is* partly us. Those first few months as a single parent are killers. Caught up in the everyday realities of life, newly divorced moms may have little strength left over to deal with the emotional traumas involved in building a new lifestyle.

The fabric of that new structure may be fragile at first, easily torn by barbed criticism or unrealistic pressures. It is not uncommon for the slightest disagreements with an ex-spouse to quickly turn into major battles. Even normal actions of the former spouse may be perceived as being deliberate attempts to harass or hurt the other. Fortunately, as time passes and the lifestyle becomes more established, both partners tend to mellow and become able to relate more openly.

If you often find yourself angry at your son's father, you may want to do a self-evaluation. Are you making unrealistic demands? Are you being inflexible? Are the issues worth getting angry over? Are you making allowances for the fact that your ex-spouse may be having difficulty getting over the breakup? Do you realize how much control you are letting your former spouse have over your life by triggering your anger? Instead of resolving conflicts and letting them go, are you stacking one "failure" on top of another, so that each new "offense" makes you more angry? Are you willing to wipe the slate clean and start over?

Letting go of the marital relationship with a former spouse is often complicated by the fact that the parenting relationship has not been severed and results in continued contact. But you *can* be successful, if you acknowledge the discomfort of your new role and understand that it will become easier as it becomes more familiar. As you recognize negative feelings and take positive action to replace them with productive activity and realistic expectations, and as you act in choice instead of anger, you will begin to feel good about your new role. It is also helpful if you focus on the future, deal with only one problem at a time, and take time out to enjoy yourself.

SOMETIMES THERE IS A CHANGE IN CUSTODY

One of the biggest fears expressed by single moms I talk with is that their sons will want to go live with their fathers some day, and that is a very real possibility. Most children like to think that they have an alternative place to live whenever things get tough at home, and where more likely than with Dad? There is more to it than that. Most boys want to have a good relationship with their fathers and want to spend some time living with them, particularly as they become adolescents and realize that they are growing up and soon will be men themselves. Also, there is often a real desire to know what the other parent is like.

The situation is similar to that experienced by adoptive parents when their adopted sons suddenly say they would like to get to know their "real parents." I believe there is an innate curiosity about who we are and where we came from that ties us to our parents and makes us want to know all about them as we grow up. The adoptive parent might feel hurt and respond by saying, "But, I *am* your real parent. I brought you home from the hospital. I have raised you and provided everything for you. I love you. Why am I not enough? Why do you need another set of parents?" Single moms who are faced with a proposed change in custody often experience those same feelings. It is hard to understand that the desire to find out about the other parent is not rejection.

I know from personal experience. I had custody of my two sons for the first six years after I was divorced. My former husband and I had a good relationship and the boys were allowed to call and visit him, but I never expected them to go live with him. I had a long list of reasons why I should continue to have custody. Then my oldest turned thirteen, and our family life became a disaster. For the next eight months he broke every rule and agreement we had, became destructive around the house, refused to participate in family activities, and got into trouble at school and in the community. Nothing I did made things better, they only got worse. Finally a counselor helped us get to the bottom of things. Jon had been trying to get me angry enough to hit him so he could call the police and charge me with abuse. Then the authorities would take him away from me and give him to his father. He was actually furious because I wouldn't hit him!

When I realized what was behind his actions, I knew that he needed to live with his father since he had been willing to go to such lengths to do so. Of course, during all of this time he hadn't bothered to discuss a change in custody with me, assuming that I wouldn't let him go willingly. And I wouldn't have.

Since his dad was pleased to have Jon live with him, things were going well for Jon, but not for me. I felt rejected, hurt, angry, and a thousand other negative feelings. It took a lot of work for me to come to the point of forgiveness, but I had learned my lesson. I told my younger son that I knew that he too would probably want to go live with his dad. While I wanted him to stay for a couple more years with me, I wasn't going to fight him about a change of custody. He agreed easily, stayed a couple of years, then went to live with his dad. That move was no problem for me as I had prepared myself for it long in advance.

But there was more. Having had custody of the boys for six years, I remembered how they used to rush to the mailbox to see if there was a letter from their dad. Now I made sure there were letters from me. I called each week. I sent them gifts, pictures, cards, and anything else I could to remind them that I loved them. By letting them go, I was able to ensure that they had a good relationship with both parents. It took work on my part, but it was worth it.

The next few years brought new challenges. At fifteen, Jon ran away from his dad and showed up at my front door saying he wanted to move back in with me. He stayed for a month then moved into an apartment with a friend. That lasted a month before he returned to his father's home. At seventeen, Jon called me from Florida, broke and hungry, asking could he come back to my house? He did, only to get into a few skirmishes with the law before, finally at age nineteen, he seemed to wake up to reality. He got a job, settled down, and began to get his life together.

Mike's story was similar. He also came back to live

with me a couple of times before he too moved out on his own.

Both boys are working steadily today, are married to lovely girls, and are struggling along with most of America to make financial ends meet.

WHEN DAD IS NOT THERE, FIND A SUBSTITUTE

Because the boys' father lived too far away for frequent visits (his home was over eight hundred miles from ours) during the early years after our divorce, I knew Jon and Mike needed additional men in their lives. I hired male sitters, signed them up for Little League, swimming, and diving teams with male coaches, and found a man in the church with sons who would include one or both of my boys in some of their "men only" activities such as camping, fishing, and hiking.

You may want to take some of these steps to build good male role models into your sons' lives.

YOUR SONS AND THE OTHER MEN IN YOUR LIFE

When there is a lack of romantic partner in your life, even the best supportive network of friends will seem inadequate at times. Apart from the general loneliness of being adrift in the unfamiliar waters of singleness, there exists a distinct longing to love and be loved by a person of the opposite sex. That longing varies from single to single. Gina wants companionship, while Sarah enjoys dating. Rhonda desires a lasting relationship, and Mary dreams of marriage.

Whether it is companionship, love, or marriage that is desired, single moms often find that dating again is quite an experience. This time, there is the added consideration of the children. Because some single moms believe that a succession of different dating partners might be confusing to their children, they choose to keep their dating lives completely separate from family lives. So they meet away from the house and restrict telephone calls with and conversations about the dating partners to times when the children are not around. Other single moms take the opposite approach and immediately involve their dates with the children, almost as if auditioning the dating partners for the role of the missing parent.

In an attempt to provide male role models for her sons, Linda used to include the boys in many of her dates. Then one day she was embarrassed when a business associate stopped by the house for some work papers and her six-year-old son asked innocently, "Are you going to be my daddy this week?"

Then Linda realized that perhaps she was trying so hard she was confusing her sons. There is no reason not to include the boys in activities with your male friends. And if your relationship with one particular man becomes serious, your sons should certainly be involved. However, problems can arise when there is a series of semi-intimate, romantic relationships. Each mom has to find the level of interaction she feels is appropriate for her dates and her sons and must consider what message she is giving her sons about male-female relationships.

Children react in different ways to a parent's active dating schedule. They are often torn between a desire to reunite their parents and the idea of helping one (or both) of the parents find a new mate. Therefore, they can be hostile to or supportive of parental dates, and their behaviors can swing from one extreme to another without warning. A sensitive parent will recognize these behaviors as cries for reassurance and will provide the extra love and attention needed. She will also discuss appropriate standards of behavior toward her dates and not allow the children to be rude or obnoxious. Even when caught up in the excitement of a new romance, she will want to be sure to give the children "equal time" and not give in to the temptation of spending all free time with the new love.

As our children observe us in a dating relationship, they will learn a lot from us. Andrea believes that all men are turkeys. Her father abused her as a child; her husband left her for a very young woman; and in two recent relationships, she was rejected just as she started to get serious. She carries a thinly veiled, heavy load of anger that she directs toward any man she gets to know well enough to risk openness with. It is no wonder that men walk away from her and that her fifteen-year-old son, Nelson, has no friends of his own sex. Our sons often pick up our attitudes.

Andrea needs to do some work in the area of forgiveness before both she and Nelson can get on with their lives. As parents we cannot afford the luxury of unresolved bitterness in our lives, because we will often end up poisoning not only our own lives but also our children's.

What are you teaching your children by your dating behavior? In what ways are you encouraging your son to relate well to his dad and to other men in general?

WHAT IF YOU REMARRY?

If you do fall in love and plan to marry again, you will want to be sensitive to the impact this will have on your son. Do some reading on stepparenting and step-relationships (see Appendix C). No matter how carefully you have protected your son from assuming the "man-of the-house" role, having a new man move into a home in a position of leadership and authority will be seen by your son as threatening to some degree. Allow your new husband and your son to develop their own unique relationship. A stepfather may be just what your son needs, but developing a good relationship may take a little time.

Chapter
6

SELF-ESTEEM
I Feel Like Such a Failure at Times!

A few years ago I decided to buy a personal computer and a printer. Because I didn't know much about the different models, I relied heavily on the advice of a couple of friends who had worked with computers for some time and were satisfied with what they had purchased. I ended up with very good bargains, a Brand A computer and a Brand B printer. The price was right and I was assured that the Brand B printer worked with the Brand A computer. I was told they were "compatible."

In the next few weeks I experienced a tremendous amount of frustration. Often I regretted ever buying a computer. I even went so far as to pack up the computer and printer intending to return them. They wouldn't do what I wanted them to! What I wanted was to bring home my new "toys," unpack them, quickly scan the instruction manual, and be able to start using them immediately. In reality, things went differently.

First, I learned that while the printer was "compatible" with the computer, I had to get a new software program that would translate the signals from the computer to this particular printer. The computer had to learn some new ways of communicating in order to be understood by the printer.

Second, if I wanted the computer and printer to do my bidding, I had to learn the commands to give and the buttons to push in correct sequence. When they did what I wanted, I was thrilled with my machines. But when they didn't, not only was I upset but I also discovered that it was usually my fault. I had done something wrong; I'd either forgotten or not known how to do the right thing.

One day I realized how similar my expectations and responses to my computer and printer were to those I had for my sons. Somewhere along the way I had picked up some strange ideas. What I seemed to have wanted was to have a son, bring him home, set him up in his room, and immediately start to see him do what I wanted, when I wanted it, the way I wanted it done!

At first, being a young mother with a baby in the house was great fun, though exhausting. Nevertheless, as the years went by, I had to learn new ways to communicate, new ways to present my commands, and new sequences for getting what I needed from my son. When he did what I wanted, I was happy and proud. When he didn't, I was frustrated and angry, sometimes fantasizing about wanting to "send him back."

There are three major differences in these experiences, however. First, when the computer and printer failed to do my bidding, it was usually my error; but when my son failed to do my bidding, it might have been my error, his error, or no one's error. People, both old and young, think for themselves and make choices about what to do or not to do.

Next, my child is not a possession who exists solely to do my bidding. He is a person, entrusted to my care for me to train to become a mature, independent adult. He will never, nor should he, become my clone.

Last, if I was particularly frustrated with trying to use my machines I could cover them up and ignore them until I was ready to try again. But when things aren't going well with my son, I still have to keep trying to connect, because it usually isn't appropriate to just stop communicating for a week or two. That's not to say, however, that a little psychological space isn't needed at times to regain a perspective and reduce the intensity of a conflict.

The conflict between mother and son tends to focus on the differences in who each person is and what is wanted or valued by each. When my son doesn't make the choices I want him to, I experience a loss of self-esteem and feel that I must have failed as a parent. When he feels that I disapprove of him simply because he isn't everything I want him to be, he also experiences a loss of self-esteem.

One afternoon when Jon was about nine, he came home late for dinner, and I was waiting with a lecture. How could he scare me that way? Didn't he know that I always came home and prepared dinner right away? Didn't he care how hard I tried to do things for him? How could he forget to check the time just because he was at a friend's house playing? I was just getting wound up, when he looked at me with his big brown eyes and explained, "Mom, I can't help it if I'm not perfect. I'm just a little boy!"

He was right. Sometimes I couldn't help feeling inadequate trying to raise my sons alone, because I never was a little boy! How was I to understand how a little boy felt or thought or why he behaved the way he did?

DON'T THINK OF YOURSELF AS INADEQUATE!

Develop a positive self-esteem: the way you feel about yourself, your overall judgment of how well you like your own particular person. As a parent you want to do everything you can to assist your son in developing a healthy self-esteem, which is linked to the mental picture you have of yourself.

Josh McDowell talks about this mental image in his book *His Image, My Image*. He says that some of us have photos of ourselves we are pleased with, which we display in silver frames of top of the piano. But many of us also have different pictures of ourselves that we hide in our wallets and only show when required to do so to cash a check, because we hate the way we look in that photo. All too often the inner mental picture we carry around looks more like the driver's license photo than the one in a silver frame. Our mental image (sometimes called our self-image) reflects what we tell ourselves about ourselves.

Your son's self-image will influence his choice of friends, how he interacts with others, whom he chooses to marry, and how productive he will be in society. It will affect his stability, his integrity, and even his creativity. In fact, his self-image has a direct bearing on all aspects of his life. Knowing how important a self-concept can be to your son, you will want to do everything you can to help him to develop *positive self-images*.

WHERE DOES SELF-ESTEEM COME FROM?

Our self-esteem has two foundations, as explained by Maurice Wagner in *The Sensation of Being Somebody*. One is *functional* and has three aspects. The aspect of *appearance* is how well we look and appear to others. The aspect of *performance* is how well we do things, our levels of skills, knowledge, and abilities. The aspect of *status* is the level of respect or importance we have from our jobs, friends, education, or family name.

The second foundation is much more significant to us because it contains our *feelings*, three of which are most important: *belongingness, worthiness,* and *competence*. Belongingness is a sense of being wanted, accepted, and cared for. Feelings of worthiness are the result of doing what we know to be right in the eyes of others. Competence is feeling adequate in a given situation because of a proven ability in similar instances.

The problems with using this approach alone in developing a positive self-image are many. Our inherent value as a human being isn't based on what we look like, how well we perform, or what status we have achieved. Belongingness depends on the voluntary acceptance of others, which may be capriciously withheld at times. Worthiness is dependent upon proper self-appraisal and approval. And competence demands success in prior endeavors. So on any given day, we can feel good or bad about ourselves based on what we think that day and how others are responding to us.

The best basis for a positive self-image is a spiritual one. We can feel great about ourselves when we come to recognize that we belong to God who has *accepted* us (see Eph. 1:6). We are considered *worthy* because Jesus Christ came to teach us about love and to pay the price for our shortcomings (see 1 Pet. 1:18–19). We are *competent* because God gives us the strength for any task (see Phil. 4:13; Deut. 33:25). Each of us has unique gifts and abilities that make us special (see 1 Cor. 12:7).

WAYS TO ENCOURAGE YOUR SON TOWARD SELF-ESTEEM

An old friend we hadn't seen in several years came to dinner one evening when Michael was about twelve. As the conversation drifted into "remember when's," Michael took an unusually active part. In fact, he became so animated he nearly took over the conversation completely. Our friend kept expressing genuine surprise that Michael could remember so far back, even events that we adults had forgotten. After about an hour when our friend went to the restroom, I whispered to Michael that he should not talk so much and bother our friend.

"But, Mom," he explained excitedly, "I'm not bothering him, I am *amazing* him!"

I understood. I relaxed and let Michael share all he

wanted to. It is one of life's rare, great thrills to have another person genuinely impressed with or admiring of us. Approval is such a treat! We all need to be affirmed and encouraged because it not only builds self-esteem, but it also reinforces a positive self-image.

Be An Affirming Mom

Not only do we need to ensure that our sons develop the spiritual aspects of a positive self-image, but we need also to provide for their identified needs for approval. Ways to affirm your son include praise, giving physical affection, listening, spending time together, allowing input into family decisions, and many other actions that we will explore more fully.

1. One Characteristic at a Time

Sally worked out a terrific plan for herself and her three sons. She made a list of twelve positive characteristics she wanted to develop in their family: love, joy, peacemaking, kindness, patience, self-control, gentleness, cheerfulness, assertiveness, consideration, dependability, and honesty. Then she assigned one, starting with kindness, to each of the twelve months. First, she and the boys discussed what kindness was and ways they could be kind to others. Then she explained that every evening at dinner for the next month they would share ways they had been kind to someone.

The first few days were the hardest. One or the other of the three would have forgotten to do a specific kind deed. But by the end of the week, all three had a story to share. "Sometimes the stories were comical, but I couldn't laugh," Sally remembered. "One day eight-year-old Kyle said he had been standing in the lunch line at school when he remembered that he needed to do something kind, so he stepped out of line and let everyone else go in first just so he could do his kind deed!"

When Sally added the second characteristic, patience, the next month the boys still shared about the kind deeds they had done. But now they included ways they had practiced patience.

Sally's plan was terrific. It gave family members a chance to share good things about themselves and be affirmed by other family members. It promoted healthful, positive conversation at dinner and encouraged new, good habits. Psychologists tell us that if we do a new behavior everyday for twenty-one days, we will develop a habit. Sally planned to develop twelve good "habits" in each family member's life over a period of a year.

You might decide to use Sally's idea. Look through the scriptures and list characteristics Christians are supposed to develop. Then practice them with your sons. Both you and the boys will be growing spiritually.

2. Setting Goals

Betty developed a "Life Notebook" with her son, Lance. When he was thirteen they made a list of everything he needed or wanted to learn to do in order to live on his own by age eighteen. The list included cooking, cleaning, washing clothes, balancing a checkbook, applying for jobs, driving a car, developing a budget. They wrote each item on the list on a separate sheet of notebook paper and put them all in a binder.

They spent weeks organizing the notebook, setting dates for the mastering of each skill, noting ways to achieve each goal, and clarifying how they would know when each skill was acquired (e.g., did family wash for one month without wrinkling the wash and wear, mixing the colored and white clothes, or having any laundry mishaps). It was a great experience just to plan the notebook, but even more fulfilling was to work through the plan and see her son develop the skills. Each time he could write Done on a page, his self-concept grew to include that skill. How's that for bringing home *management by objectives* principles!

You may not want to be quite that elaborate, but it is wise to assist your son in setting and achieving goals. Goals provide a direction and purpose for channeling activity. Achieving goals provides a sense of accomplishment that is a wonderful boost to one's self-esteem. Remember how good it feels to check off the completed items on your Saturday to-do list? Help your son learn the joy of accomplishment by encouraging him to set and achieve good goals.

Working on goals together will give you and your son opportunities to get to know one another better as people and not just as parent and child. Spending positive time with someone is also a good way of affirming worth as an individual and further builds self-esteem.

Before setting goals together as a family, take time to read the Bible together to get God's goals in mind. There are lots of instructions in the Word that give straightforward guidelines, but almost any passage can be used to identify God's standards for His children. For our children, the stories are sometimes easier to identify with than direct instructions. First Corinthians 10:11–13 tells us that we can learn from the experiences of the Israelites. Read a story together and then discuss how the characters behaved and the consequences of their choices. Discuss how the same types of choices are presented to us each day. Help your children decide on proper choices and then try to find ways to practice the new, correct choices.

3. Family Night Activities

"I'd love to go to the party with you, Diane," Sharon told her friend. "But I can't. I'm already committed for Tuesday. That's family night at our house."

"Family night! That's only for your kids. Can't you change it just this once?" Diane coaxed teasingly.

"No. Family night is a priority in our home," Sharon answered seriously.

Having a family night at your house can be a very special way of becoming, or staying, close to your children. Plans for fun things to do for family nights can be found in many books and magazines at bookstores or libraries if you run short of ideas yourself (see Appendix C).

When you first start having family nights, you may find the new schedule difficult, but if you don't give up and keep your commitment to developing your family uppermost in your mind, you will soon find that you wouldn't miss family nights for the world! Besides, the nights are affirming if you give them priority, because you are saying by your actions that your children are important to you. And they will know and feel that they are loved.

4. By Word and Deed

"Sometimes I feel as if I never have anything positive to say to my children," Ellen said. "Between the 'don'ts,' the 'no's,' and the 'stop that's,' I rarely get a chance to catch my breath, let alone tell my children how well they are doing!"

If we want to act as loving guides and affirm the development of our sons, we need to be truly committed to being available when needed, to offering support and encouragement when the going gets tough, and to providing the discipline that is needed. Here are a few suggestions others have found helpful:

- Find one thing each day to affirm in your son. At first this may be difficult if you are not used to complimenting your son, but the affirmation need not be something major, just something you appreciate: a clean room, the outfit chosen to wear to school, helping with the dishes, taking out the trash, or cheerfully running an errand.

- Express your personal confidence in the child. At least three or four times a week express your belief that your son can accomplish something. This is best if it is something the child has set as a goal, but it is also valuable if it is about something the child doesn't think is possible. Be sure to be honest so that your confidence in the child becomes something to be trusted, not false praise. "You can do it" and "You did that very well" are wonderful affirmations, if they are true. Reflect on how good you feel when a friend believes that you can successfully take on a big project, or the boss entrusts you with a special job. You seem to grow with and rise to the occasion. You feel increased self-esteem as you recognize that someone else has confidence in you. Give your son that same experience.

- Don't be too hasty with a no. If your first instinct

is to say no when your child asks to do something different, try a few more yeses. Risk taking is a part of growing up and your child should not be deprived of stretching and growing. This, of course, does not mean you shouldn't take proper safety precautions, if indicated.

• Allow your son the freedom to fail without heaping incriminations on his head. Part of risking is learning to take failures in stride.

As the two of you focus on the positives, you will find that your son will begin to develop more independence and maturity, which is one of the goals of parenting. And most likely, along the way, you will have grown a bit yourself.

5. Listen

Nancy shared, "I find that when Donny has something on his mind and I invite him to share, he really appreciates my listening. I mean, I stop what I am doing and sit down so I can give him my full attention. That is one way I can let him know how much I care."

Nancy is right. Attentive listening is an important way to build another person's self-esteem, to show that he or she is valued. Nancy continued, "Whenever I am tempted not to give Donny my full attention, I remember an experience I had with a girl friend. When we used to talk on the telephone it was like talking to her whole family, including the dog. She would turn away from the phone and carry on a conversation with one or the other or both of her children, laugh at the dog's antics, and seem to pay attention to everyone else except me. I used to feel as if I weren't important enough for her to give me her full attention for the few minutes we were talking on the telephone. I don't want my son to feel that way about me."

6. Recognize His Right to Be Unique

"Every once in a while I have to remind myself that Fred has a right to be his own person," Patricia said. "We don't have to like the same clothes, music, television shows, movies, books, jokes, friends, or foods. I have a lot of friends who don't like some of the same things I do and that's okay. It needs to be okay for my son not to as well."

Why is it so hard for us to acknowledge the differences between us and our sons? I believe the reason is that we think people will judge us by our children's choices—and they may! But each one of us is unique, an unrepeatable miracle, designed to be different. So unless our sons' choices are harmful to themselves or others, we must let them do the choosing.

We must begin to appreciate the individual differences in our sons in order to appreciate them fully. We are not alike, but we can complement one another and form a strong, working, family team.

PROTECT YOUR OWN SELF-ESTEEM

You will find that as you consciously do the things described in this chapter to build your son's self-esteem, in the process you will have begun to feel good about yourself as a parent. However, don't let all your self-esteem depend upon your role as a parent, for you are a total person. You will recognize that you are a loving, caring, kind, understanding, affirming, achieving, wonderful person!

If that's true, then why is it that we sometimes feel as if we are failures? Perhaps we haven't taken care of some of our own support and *belonging* needs. It helps to join a singles group, get involved in activities at church, participate in the PTA or other community activities, get a job, and cultivate a few good friendships, particularly with other single moms.

Maybe you need to work on your feelings of *worthiness* by reflecting on the many ways you are doing the best you know how as a person and a parent. Share with good friends about difficult areas in your life where you are sticking to your guns regardless of the cost, and reflect on the people who depend on you for something in their lives, such as friendship, shelter, joy, laughter.

You may need to reassure yourself of your *competence* by setting and achieving goals and reminding yourself of positive accomplishments, by reviewing the many areas in which you have been successful, and by making a list of your strengths.

Most of all, you need a strong personal faith and an active spiritual life to maintain a proper self-image. In addition, there are other things you can do.

Take Time Alone

A common fantasy of single moms with custody of their children is having some uninterrupted time alone! How that time would be spent varies from individual to individual. You may dream of reading, relaxing, sitting on the patio, studying, working on a favorite hobby, sleeping, or just doing nothing. When asked about the obstacles to living out such fantasies, several moms cited guilt about being selfish, having too many other priorities, or not having anyone to

97

watch the children. And so, failing to overcome such obstacles, too many of us dutifully focus on our parenting role to the exclusion of other areas of our lives.

There is a time when I dreaded going home after work because I was always greeted at the door by both boys, each making several demands at once. Finally, I resolved this problem by negotiating with the kids. They agreed that for the first thirty minutes after I came home they would leave me alone. No questions, no demands. The second half hour I would talk with and listen to them. That quiet thirty minutes each day made a significant difference in our relationships.

Whether it is thirty minutes a day, one evening a week, or even an occasional weekend without the children, you must decide what will meet your needs. Then work out the details.

Get a Hug

When was the last time you received a friendly bear hug when you needed it? More and more single adults are discovering the value of friendly hugs. That comforting, affirming, nonsexual touch from another adult often says, You can do it! I care! I understand! Hang in there!

Words of encouragement are important. A sympathetic ear is comforting. But there's nothing like being held. Become a hugger. Each time you give a hug, you get a hug back. So, the more you give, the more you get. Learn to tell a good friend that you need a hug.

If you are one of those people who aren't comfortable with physical touching, you can "get in touch" with others in different ways. You can call a friend and go out together for coffee. Or you can send cards or write letters.

Even if you don't enjoy physical closeness with other adults, you are probably affectionate with the children. You will want to express your love in the family with a lot of touching, particularly during tough times. A hug or a hand on the shoulder says much more than words can. If you have never developed the habit of affectionate touching within your family, start now. It may take a while, but you will soon become comfortable.

You and your sons can give each other an affirming "touch" by playing physical contact sports, romping, mock wrestling, giving piggyback rides, brushing one another's hair. Perhaps you will want to trade backrubs, crowd into a hottub, or cuddle up under a blanket and tell scary stories.

We need one another. We are social beings. So as the familiar advertising jingle says, "Reach out and touch someone."

Get Professional Assistance if Needed

There were times when I needed professional help, so I called a counselor to make an appointment. When the frustration, pain, and uncertainty made me question my approach, I went for help, confirmation, and advice.

When you are facing specific major problems or can't seem to cope with the consistent realities of single-again life, a counselor's office is usually the best place to go for advice, guidance, and assistance. One of the most frequent reasons single moms consult counselors is that there are problems with the children. Discipline is a big issue because children who have not sorted out their feelings, adjusted to the breakup, or developed the skills to cope with trauma, may act up as a result of those fears, hostilities, or insecurities.

It is important to remember that whenever one family member has a problem of this nature, it becomes a family problem. No one suffers alone. Most of these behaviors or symptoms are a cry for help or a response to a situation that is perceived as intolerable. Don't let these problems make you feel that you are a failure as a parent. Don't let your self-image slip down. And don't let a lack of money prevent you from seeking professional assistance if it is needed by you or your children. Get help.

Several resources are probably available to you. School districts often have free family counseling services. Your medical insurance may cover counseling. Many pastors or lay church leaders serve as volunteer counselors. The local social services department may be of assistance. There may be a women's center in your town.

Seeking professional assistance when needed is the wisest move a mom can make when the family experiences troubled times. It is not a sign of weakness, but one of strength.

Develop a Strong Personal Relationship with the Lord

Your secret strength, not only for the parenting job but also for being successful in life, is to develop a strong, personal relationship with the Lord. You need His guidance every day in your life, and you need the Word on a daily basis. Become involved in a Bible study program either on Sunday or during the week. Take time for personal devotions. Seek the fellowship of other Christians, particularly single moms raising sons alone. These can give you the strength, the wisdom, the support, and the joy you need to be a good, Christian mom.

Most of all, be gentle with yourself. You are doing the best that you can. If there's something you don't really like about your approach to parenting, start now to change. Do it slowly, one step at a time. As human beings we have the ability to choose to make changes. We can learn and grow.

Chapter

7

VALUES

I Know What I Want My Son to Become

The moments when I've felt the most fulfilled as a parent are when one of my sons shows signs of adopting my values or beliefs. Conversely, my deepest disappointments have been when they've chosen to reject my value system.

Not long ago I sat alone in my bedroom, emotionally raw and bleeding after a discussion with my younger son, then nineteen years old.

How, I asked myself, *could I have raised a son to have values so different from mine? Where have I gone wrong?* I felt like such a failure.

Our talk had been calm as he discussed his beliefs about a parent's financial responsibility to a son. From my perspective his views were bizarre, totally contrary to mine, and would probably ensure his failure to stand on his own within the predictable future. Because I didn't agree that I should support him while he sat around and spent money he didn't have for things he didn't need, he quietly labeled me as unloving and unnatural. Even though I knew that one day he would change his mind, I hurt.

There usually comes a time when we must test the levels of our love and acceptance of our sons when they choose values that are very different from ours and the ones we want them to choose.

King David must have felt that same way. Remember David's son, Absalom? As a young man Absalom had his servants kill his brother Amnon. Rightfully afraid of King David's wrath, Absalom fled the country and five years passed before David would see or speak to his son. When he did, they were reconciled. But Absalom, far from being grateful, spent the next forty years trying to undermine his father's authority. During that time the Bible says he "stole the hearts of the men of Israel." Absalom was a real con man. Finally he launched a successful rebellion, usurped the throne, and moved into a tent on top of Kind David's own home, forcing David to flee for his life. Yet when King David prepared his battle plan, he ordered his generals to deal gently with Absalom. The soldiers disobeyed and killed Absalom instead. When King David heard the news, he was heartbroken, crying, "Oh my son, Absalom, my son, my son. Would God I had died for you!" His *son* was over sixty years old and had spent many years in rebellion against law and order and his father, yet David still cried. He must have wondered how a son of his could have chosen such a destructive value system.

The stronger our own value system is the more compelled we feel to instill that same system in our sons, particularly when our values spring from a firmly held faith. We can expect to experience confusion and conflict until we have established a set of beliefs to put order into such areas of our lives as politics, religion, family, friends, work, leisure, love, sex, male/female roles, race, poverty, energy, health, money, personal habits, drugs, education, and on and on!

Wanting to pass on our values is part of our Christian heritage, part of our God-given responsibility, and most of us take it seriously. Ever since the beginning of the human family, God has expected us as parents to try and communicate our values to our sons. God commanded the Israelites to commemorate the Passover every year after the exodus from Egypt and to tell their children how He had saved them from slavery (Ex.12:26). Throughout the Old Testament parents were instructed to pass on the story of what God had done. In the New Testament, Timothy was a good example and his mother and grandmother were given credit for his developing a strong, genuine faith (2 Tim.1:5). If there were just one thing I could pass on to my sons, it would be my faith. Next in importance come my values. I have often claimed Proverbs 22:6, which tells me that if I train up my children in the ways they should go, when they are old, they will not depart from those ways. I hope they live to be old enough to do just that.

How can we help our sons cope with the confusing and conflicting messages they are constantly receiving from people whose value systems differ from ours? One way is to *tell* them what to do and think, how to distinguish right from wrong, good from bad. Most of us use this approach at times, particularly when our sons are very young. As they grow older we tend to progress from ordering to persuading to advising. Those mothers who remain in the ordering phase find that at some point their sons rebel against an authoritative approach. They also discover that just telling sons something in no way ensures that they will accept it as true for them, even if they comply with what they are told. If *telling* worked, we would all be perfect, because we too have been *told* how to behave by our teachers, preachers, parents, neighbors, and books.

A second way to communicate our value system is to *model* what we want our sons to think and do. Most of us try to live according to what we believe is right, but few of us manage always to live up to our own standards. Our sons are very quick to spot the inconsistencies. Also, our sons are exposed to many models (teachers, friends, public figures, television characters) who often model conflicting values, goals, lifestyles, speech patterns, moral codes, and orientations toward work and play, life and death. So which models will they choose to follow? It may not be ours, no matter how hard we try to influence their choices.

Pam and Sid were both well educated (he had a Ph.D. in Education and she a Masters degree in Business Administration) and held good jobs where they were each considered reliable and competent. Nevertheless, both of their sons dropped out of high school and had such poor work habits they had difficulty holding jobs. Pam and Sid were puzzled and disappointed. How could they have failed to pass on their values about education and work to their sons? Finally, they had to acknowledge that there are no guarantees that their children would adopt their values.

When we tell our sons our values, we find that we

are competing with everyone else's messages and the boys may not even be listening. When we model our values, we cross our fingers, hoping and praying that our sons are watching. Some are; others are not. Some boys grow into adulthood filled with contradictory values and inconsistent beliefs and behaviors. Depending upon the persuasiveness of others, they are easily enticed into points of view and actions contrary to our desires. We could despair of teaching values at all. But there is still another approach.

A third way to assist our sons to develop their value system is to *discuss values and their impact on our lives.* We really can help influence some of the values our sons choose. (A value is a belief that, after careful consideration, has been selected from various choices and is acted upon repeatedly and consistently over a period of time.) We all have values. Through the process of considering several other options and perhaps even experiencing by trial and error some of the consequences of the options, we take a particular belief and make it truly our own.

Bill had been taught at an early age that stealing was wrong. He never took candy from the local grocery store, never stole a toy, never slipped money out of his mom's purse. He followed what he had been told was right, until he was sixteen. Then he and several friends stole a car and were arrested.

Sitting in jail the next few hours, Bill evaluated his decision to go along with the boys' stealing the car. He decided that he didn't like the consequences and that he would never steal again. And he didn't—not so much as a pencil from the office. Until he was sixteen, Bill followed his mother's values. Then, after choosing honesty for himself, he lived by his own value system.

The more we can involve our sons in making life decisions by having them consider the options and consequences before they make a choice, the better chance we will have of helping them develop a well-defined value system. It is important that we not be the person who is always administering the consequences, or our sons' value systems may become to obey mom until she no longer has the power to enforce consequences. We must help our sons see the larger picture when considering the consequences of various choices.

The valuing process has several dimensions.

1. Thinking Is One Aspect of Developing Values

In order to teach my sons how to reason things through, I started asking them to come up with pros and cons for an issue or choice we might be discussing. At age ten, when Jon was planning how to buy a motorcycle when he was old enough to ride one, he was full of ideas about the good things about motorcycles. When I asked him to give me reasons why buying a motorcycle might be a bad choice, he was stumped at first. Then hesitantly, he began to mention rain, no room for passengers, no big trunk, and danger on the highways. He was beginning to learn that there are always two sides to any issue. We played this game for the next several years. I was delighted to begin to see the boys sometimes bringing me well-thought-out ideas after they learned how to consider both sides.

The more we can stimulate our sons to think by capturing their imagination and encouraging them to stretch their mental limits, the better off they will be.

Try to eliminate mindless behaviors and choices. Watching television together? After a show ask, "Why do you suppose the character acted the way he did?" Or, "What made that scene so funny to us?" Or, "How would you have handled that and why?"

Teaching our sons to think well is a big task but a very important one. Proverbs 23:7 says that as we think in our hearts, we are. What we think influences how we feel about an issue and how we act in a situation. If we can help our sons learn to think clearly, we are giving them a gift beyond price.

2. Feelings Influence Our Values

Jon was twelve when he first experienced rejection from a girl. He liked her so much and she had told him he was boring! He was so hurt. Through tears he was fighting to hold back, he vowed never to like a girl again because he wouldn't be liked in return. There have been times when I felt the same way when I have been rejected. But both Jon and I have reevaluated our feelings and realized that our beliefs about being unlovable were inaccurate.

We feel strongly about the values we hold most dear. When your son is angry or hurt or ecstatic, ask him to verbalize what belief has been rejected or affirmed by someone else. This helps him to learn to identify his beliefs as the bases of his emotional responses.

3. Choosing Is a Vital Step

When we set goals and gather information about the various ways to achieve our goals, we review and consider the options and consequences before choosing a direction to pursue. If we have a goal to improve our standard of living, we consider ways to get more money (take a second job, try for a promotion, change jobs or careers, inherit a million dollars, or win the state lottery). After reviewing all of the possibilities, we may decide that a college degree would help us qualify for a promotion, so we enroll in classes. We know how to use the choosing process.

When fourteen-year-old Lou said he wanted to become a mechanical engineer, his mom encouraged him to research the requirements, job market, average salary levels, and colleges offering the right degree. She found a mechanical engineer at church who was willing to come to their home to talk about his career with Lou. One night she and Lou discussed what it was about engineering that interested Lou and listed other careers that might provide the same things. After a few weeks of active consideration, Lou was sure of his choice. He might have changed his mind as his values were being explored. But having made his choice, he was then able to base subsequent decisions on that choice. He did his homework faithfully *in order to* keep his grades up, *in order to* qualify for a scholarship for the college of his choice, *in order to* become an engineer. Although the decision was his, part of his eventual success as an engineer was due to a mother who took the time to help him make that personal choice a firm one.

If we can assist our sons in making good choices, they will usually be turning away from bad choices. Often right and wrong choices are so diametrically opposed that one can't choose them both. Matthew 6:19–24 outlines this principle. We cannot serve two masters: We cannot choose both God's way and the world's way. Thus, if we can assist them in choosing well, we can shout with Joshua, "As for me and my family, we will serve the Lord!" (Josh. 24:15).

4. Communicating About Our Values Reinforces Them

Values do not develop in a vacuum but through an ongoing process of sound interaction. The more we explain our beliefs, the more feedback we receive and the more information we have from which to make good choices. Discussion and conflict resolution are powerful ways to strengthen our values.

One day twelve-year-old Ernie came home and announced that he was going to quit school as soon as he was sixteen because school was a waste of time. Instead of ignoring his statement or hitting the ceiling, his mom stopped what she was doing to discuss the issue with him. She asked him to make a list of pros and cons about quitting school and another list of pros and cons for staying in school. Then they reviewed the lists together. Although some of the pros on the quitting school list sounded ridiculous to her, Mom didn't laugh. She gave her honest feedback about what he had written. Then she asked Ernie to think of other adults whose opinions he respected. Together they picked three from the list and Ernie agreed to share his lists with and get feedback from those people within the next few days. Ernie also was to explore the job opportunity market for people without a high school education and to validate his beliefs by talking with the vocational counselor at school and a businessman friend of the family. Eventually Ernie decided for himself that staying in school was his better alternative. It wasn't Mom making him stay, rather he chose to stay.

We must teach our sons to communicate, to understand and verbalize well. I love the story of Jesus in the temple, amazing the teachers with his understanding and wise questions. What a goal to shoot for, to have our sons so wise they amaze others! However, I'd settle for just having the ability to communicate well, to express feelings, to share ideas, and to explain thought processes.

5. Our Actions Prove What Values We Have Chosen

Ten-year-old Mike shared his lunch with a classmate who had forgotten his lunch. After school he proudly told the story. I responded, "Sounds like being a good friend is important to you."

"Yeah," Mike said, restating his values, "I like to be nice to my friends."

As we act repeatedly and consistently upon our beliefs, our value systems become integral parts of our lives. We become skilled in those actions and feel good about ourselves in the process. When our son tells us about a good choice he has made, let's see if we can identify the positive belief he acted upon and affirm it.

Taking the right action is important. James 1:22–25 tells us that we must be doers, not just hearers of the Word in order to be doing right. And in chapter 4, verse 17, he actually says that if we know what we should do and don't do it, we are sinning! Actions are critical not only in our sons' lives, but in our own.

SEVERAL PROBLEMS YOU WILL ENCOUNTER WHEN TEACHING VALUES

"Just when I think I am making progress with my son, his dad reinforces the opposite behavior," Janet sighs. It is true that sometimes the values at the other home are not those we mothers would prefer. Dad may be lazy, financially irresponsible, a messy housekeeper, impatient or vulgar. He may even go so far as to mock the values we are trying to instill. Instead of becoming frustrated or belittling the ex-spouse, we must recognize that there is a difference in values and recognize that ultimately each son will choose his own values.

During the teenage years, a boy's friends may also be obstacles to sharing one's values with him. In anticipation of this, a mother will want to emphasize the importance of choosing the right friends, starting when the child is very young. Watch television programs together and discuss—don't preach—the values involved in the program, particularly those that involve friendships. Ask him how the story might have been different if the leading man/boy had chosen different friends. Make up stories about friendships and tell them to one another. Read stories and discuss what part friends played in the hero's life. Research what God has to say about the situation, choice, or action. Encourage him to see how his own choice of friends is helpful or harmful in various situations as he grows up.

I found that often I was uneasy with my sons' choices of friends, and I struggled with what to do.

One friend was so out-of-control that he tried to commit suicide twice in one year. Another had lost his father in an accident and was expressing his anger by destructive actions. The fourteen-year-old took his father's car and drove it around the neighborhood recklessly whenever his mother was away at work. I tried to provide different friends for the boys, who, naturally, wanted to choose their own. I felt helpless sometimes, wondering how much more influence the friends would have over my sons' choices than I would have. Part of this problem was resolved when a job change caused us to move, and I was able to get the boys involved with new friends whose values and life-styles were more similar to those I held.

There may come a time when you will have to limit the relationship with certain friends your son chooses. While you cannot prevent your teenager from spending time with undesirable friends, you can certainly make your desires known. You can also make your home off-limits to those boys, not allow your son to spend the night at their homes, and refuse to drive your son somewhere he might be meeting them. But the truth is that if he genuinely wants to spend time with someone, he will probably find a way to do so behind your back.

Sometimes more drastic measures are necessary. A friend of ours was getting in with the wrong crowd. His parents tried everything they could to influence him to choose better friends. Finally, in desperation, they moved to a different town, thirty miles away. That did the trick. The young man grew up to be a missionary and became everything his parents had hoped for him to be.

When considering the appropriateness of the friends your son is choosing, be sure you aren't confusing personal preference with moral values. It is easy to judge kids on the length or color of hair (purple, green, orange) or the style of dress they choose. Values are more enduring than temporary fads.

The third possible obstacle we may face in teaching our values to our sons may be ourselves! Actions still speak louder than words, so we need to model what we profess to believe in. Secondly, the way we present our values must not be preachy or nagging. We cannot expect our children to be carbon copies of us. They are unique persons, just as we are, and they will not necessarily be who we wish them to become. In fact, aren't we all still becoming? I know I am still working on growing up in many areas of my own life.

Probably the best approach to sharing your values with your son is to use all three methods, telling, modeling, and assisting him in making intelligent, considered choices of his own.

ADOLESCENCE IS A KEY PERIOD IN YOUR SON'S LIFE

The transition from boyhood to manhood involves some of the most significant life changes your son will ever experience. He will question values that have been imposed on him by parents and teachers. And that questioning will compel him to rethink, wrestle with, and own values he has presumed were his. During this time every aspect of life and every idea, emotion, relationship, habit, and interest he has will be affected. The postadolescent boy is as different from the preadolescent as the butterfly is different from the caterpillar.

When your son reaches adolescence, it might be helpful for you to look at the typical characteristics for this period.

The preadolescent—around age twelve—usually thinks in concrete terms. He finds abstract ideas hard to grasp because he is just beginning to be able to comprehend principles and concepts. He can answer factual questions easily but struggles with "why" questions. Often he participates in discussions on a superficial level, and he is easily distracted. He takes about twice as long to do a task as he will at age seventeen, but he can't sit still for long. His attention span depends on his interest and personal involvement with the subject, and his basic motivation is still "What's in it for me?" His moods swing often and quickly, and he will probably not be seriously interested in the opposite sex.

The postadolescent—about age seventeen—is quite different. He is able to think in abstract terms, handle principles and concepts, consider a series of facts, and draw valid conclusions. He can discuss ideas in depth and sit still for an extended period of time, but he still needs to be actively involved in working on a project or learning something new. His motivation is likely "Who else is doing it?" Emotionally he will show a great deal of stability, and he will probably be very interested in the opposite sex.

Of course, the boy won't just wake one morning as a postadolescent. The change will be gradual over the period of several years between twelve and seventeen. During this time you will have to be patient with him as he matures.

As boys mature physically, they experience a series of physical changes that are alternately fascinating and frustrating to themselves and others. This period of physical maturation is marked by transformation other than the preparation of the body for reproduction. Growth of large muscles is rapid, but the development of coordination is slow. Unaccustomed to his new body, the boy may bump into things, fall down, and need a lot of room to move about in. Also, his growth produces an explosion of energy that he must use, which makes it impossible for him to sit still for very long.

Often mothers become anxious about and impatient with the rate and direction of development, not just physically but in all ways. When parental expectations are not realized, there may be conflict with sons. Consider Tom's situation. His mom expects him to keep his room picked up daily, but Tom feels that once a week is more than enough. Therefore Sunday through Friday, Mom and Tom argue the issue, and by Saturday when Tom does clean his room, his mom's response is a frustrated, "Well, it's about time!"

The difference between what parents expect and what a teenager does is the measure of tension, anxiety, and conflict in the home (see Figure on page 117).

To reduce the tension, both mother and son will need to rethink their expectations, face each situation as it really is, and go from there. Often a workable compromise is possible. If both Tom and his mother agree that the room should be cleaned twice a week, the arguments, tension, and frustration would be eliminated. Reducing tension and frustration often opens up communications and improves relationships.

FOCUSING ON FOUR VALUES

Although there are many values parents want to pass on, there are four that seem to be universally important to mothers: honesty, caring, self-sufficiency, and a spiritual faith.

Honesty

"I can take almost anything but being lied to," Gwen said with emphasis. "I hate it when I find out I've been deceived. I feel betrayed and have a hard time ever trusting that person again."

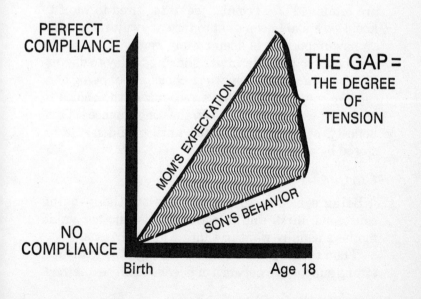

PERFECT COMPLIANCE

THE GAP = THE DEGREE OF TENSION

MOM'S EXPECTATION

SON'S BEHAVIOR

NO COMPLIANCE

Birth   Age 18

Gwen is not alone in her feelings. All of us need honest relationships in our lives with people who tell the truth and keep their word, whom we can believe and trust. Voicing the importance of honesty is the first step toward sharing this value with our sons.

Then we should discuss the importance of honesty; memorize appropriate scriptures; treat dishonesty in others as a serious issue; express our disappointment when others fail to be honest with us; and affirm honesty in others and in our sons.

The second step is to model honesty in our own lives: no cheating on income taxes, asking the kids to lie about our whereabouts to avoid unwanted telephone calls, advising a friend to call in sick when actually playing hooky from work.

Next, we need to watch for opportunities to initiate discussions with our sons regarding honesty. When we are reminded of a promise we're too tired to want to keep, we should keep the promise anyway, remarking on how important is keeping our word.

Whenever possible invite sharing of day-to-day experiences in which there was a choice about being honest. We may not even have recognized the choice to be an honesty issue. Focus on the consequences of dishonesty, of not being trusted until confidence is restored by a period of honesty.

Caring

Being sensitive to the feelings of others—being courteous, kind, and affectionate—is another value mothers usually want to share with their sons.

"I don't want Eric to blunder through life without a strong supportive network of friends," Amy explained.

"So he needs to learn to be a good friend. In fact, we have a saying in our family, 'Loving is doing.' Sometimes Eric will do something wrong and then say he loves me. I respond by saying that I love him, too, but that loving is *doing*. Usually he gets the message and tries to demonstrate his love by doing something nice."

The thirteenth chapter of 1 Corinthians is a wonderful study on what love really is and how it is manifested in our lives. Spend several evenings as a family discussing that chapter and ways you can grow toward the ideal. Discuss how God's love is an example of perfect love and how we are expected to love one another as we are loved (John 13:34–35; 1 John 4:7–10).

Although you don't want to give the impression that your love is conditional, it is important to teach your children that love takes action. Love is demonstrated by what you *do* more than by what you *say*.

After you talk about love and how important it is to be kind, you need to model that behavior yourself. Plan ways to demonstrate love for a neighbor, friend, or relative. Your family can offer to spend a Saturday helping to do yard work or cleaning their garage. You can cater a dinner for a friend or pack a basket of gifts for no particular reason and leave it on your friend's doorstep to be discovered later.

The possibilities are endless. The point is obvious. While you are working on these projects, you can talk with your sons about how much fun it is to be able to surprise people and let them know you care about them.

"Don't forget to let your children know that you show your love by your actions," Vicky said. And she was right. On the stack of freshly laundered clothes you put on your son's bed, pin a note saying, "I did your laundry because I love you and want you to have clean clothes."

When helping your son choose kindness as a value, remember that this is not the place for unrealistic expectations. None of our sons will ever be perfect. They will all fall short, as we mothers will, of the ideal. They will not always feel loving or act lovingly; the best we can hope for is that they will most of the time. Whenever your son does choose to act lovingly, let him know that you notice and encourage him. When he asks your advice on how to handle a situation, you might respond, "What would be the loving thing to do?" See if you can get him to think about the consequences of being a caring person. Encourage a caring lifestyle.

One way to teach about responsible caring is with pets. If you emphasize that a pet's life may depend on your son's feeding it and giving it fresh water, the relationship between loving and caring is manifested.

Self-sufficiency

"I don't think Tony will ever learn to take care of himself!" Carol lamented half-seriously, but half-jokingly, too. There are times when it seems as if the only hope for the kids' rooms is a fire! Perhaps your fifteen year old seems to want to starve rather than cook for himself. Or you may have a nineteen year old who has yet to go out and get a job. Carol's Tony is a good example.

Tony has held several good jobs. He interviews well and is hired easily. His problem is that he sabotages his own success. Within the first month he gets bored, becomes disillusioned with his manager, dissatisfied with company policies, or just doesn't go to work some days. Soon he is out looking for a "better job," which he usually finds and then starts the whole cycle over again. His resume shows a string of eight or nine different jobs each year. When asked about it, he just shrugs and says he's going to keep trying to get the best job he can. The problem is will he ever recognize that great job when he gets it?

Some boys sabotage their independence in other ways.

John has a good job but spends all of his money on his car, stereo, clothes, and eating out. He still lives at home because he says he can't afford an apartment.

Sam is a diabetic. He moved into his own apartment, got a job, and did well for five or six months. However, since he doesn't watch his diet, he ends up in the hospital about twice a year. Then he loses his job and apartment and moves back in with Mom until he can get a new job, save enough for an apartment, and move out again. He's twenty-eight and this pattern has gone on for years.

James knows he can live at home with his mom as long as he is in college. He is twenty-seven and still in school because he keeps changing his major.

All of these young men are refusing to assume personal responsibility for their lives and are clinging to their dependency on their mother.

Teaching Financial Independence

Lecturing your son on the merits of self-sufficiency will probably be ineffective, but that shouldn't stop you from sharing your ideas about the issue. Just don't harp on them! You may need to make changes in your own lifestyle if your financial affairs are not in order. If you are in debt and behind in your payments, your sons may adopt that lifestyle also.

If you are a new single parent, changing your lifestyle may present a special challenge. "We never go out to eat anymore!" Jeremy wailed. "And I'm sick of hot dogs!"

The single-parent family almost always experiences a change in its financial situation. In cases where both spouses had worked, half of the family income is now gone. Expenses can soar as the one parent is required to establish a new household, even if he or she is thrifty.

Single moms with custody who do not work outside of the home face such alternatives as lowering their standard of living and trying to make ends meet on whatever support is provided from the other parent or accepting some form of support from family and friends. If widowed, they must live on the former spouse's insurance or investments or else get a job.

Whatever the income, the single parent can always benefit from exploring low-cost fun and increasing the family awareness of ways to conserve money. If your family works together, you will find that you can afford that occasional night out, a vacation, or a major purchase. Enlist the family's help, and learn good money management together. You might consider making your own Christmas and birthday gifts, or perhaps you would attempt to make your own household cleaning products (see *Formula Book* by Norman Start; New York: Avon, 1976). Try conserving energy and water and watching the bills go down, or develop creative menus using inexpensive but nutritious foods. Make a list of twenty fun things to do in your town for under a dollar a person and use this list for family outings.

Unfortunately, many single parents I know have to work not only one job but two. Wendy used to hurry to her car after her day job, drive home, serve dinner in exactly fifteen minutes, change clothes, and dash off to her second job as a sales clerk in a large department store. She clerked only twenty hours a week and they did need the extra money, she kept telling herself, but she began to feel so tired she finally had to give up the second job and find other ways to solve her money problems.

For some single moms a second job is a survival measure; for others it is a way to provide a few extras for the family. Most who work a second job wonder at times if the benefits are worth the cost. Trying to hold down two jobs entails more effort than just working extra hours. There are the hidden stresses of having two bosses to please, extra travel arrangements to make, the frustration of "dead time" between the two jobs (time too short to accomplish anything but too long to waste), and another set of procedures to learn and master.

If you try to work two jobs for too long, you will become overly tired (waking up as unrested as when you went to bed); overreact to frustrations and conflicts; and overlook what's going on in the family life. The price you will pay is not only the reduction in the number of hours you have to spend with your sons, but also a little less of you to give, even when you are with them. Relaxing together will be difficult. You will be mentally preoccupied so that listening not only to what is said but also to what is meant will become an impossible challenge. Few special presents or pleasures the extra income may provide can match the value of your being able to give fully of yourself to the children. Therefore if you are considering taking a second job, take time to consider your options:

- Maybe you could get a better-paying first job.
- Try for overtime at your "first job."
- Perhaps your home is large enough to share and split expenses with another one-parent family or with a college student.
- Perhaps the children could earn their own spending money.

If, after considering all of your options, you decide that a second job is the only solution to your financial situation, then you might be able to work at home typing, telephone answering, babysitting. Or you might try a set-your-own-hours-career, such as direct sales (Avon, Amway, Shaklee, Beeline Fashions, jewelry, Tupperware). Set a goal of when you will be more secure financially and will no longer need that second job. Simplify the rest of your life and spend quality time with the boys.

One way to prepare our sons for independence is to give them an allowance and make them responsible for some of their own expenses. This can be an excellent way for children to learn money management. The Family Service Association of the Mid-Peninsula in Northern California recommends the following allowances for free spending money.

ages 7–8: $1–$2 weekly
ages 9–12: $3–4 weekly
ages 12–15: $5 weekly
ages 16+: none; it is time for an outside job

The amount of the allowance will vary from family to family, depending on the family's budget and the parent's sense of what is appropriate. An overly generous allowance defeats the purpose of the parent's giving it. After the decision is made regarding expenses the boy is going to be responsible for, parents must be firm. No advances on allowances! Usually he must pay for his own entertainment (movies, arcades, roller skating) or between meal snacks, lunches at school, or for older boys, his own clothes. The size of the allowance will depend on what it is to cover.

Some boys will immediately spend every cent on arcades, snacks, or one big purchase. Others will carefully hoard their incomes, saving for an expensive item.

Using an allowance for discipline (withholding part or all as a punishment), or as a payment for chores, is not recommended. Money for chores should be a separate transaction. When paying children their allowances, never complain about the family's financial difficulties. Many children in one parent situations are worried about money. They often daydream about having huge sums of money to give to help out with budgetary problems. Receiving their allowances should not add to their fears and concerns.

Creative budgeting can help in finding money to give the boys an allowance. Compute how much money you spend per week on snacks and reduce that amount by the amount of the allowances. Substitute a costly family outing (going out to dinner or the movies) for a cheaper one (barbecuing or renting a video). Change banks when you find one that doesn't deduct a service charge for checks. Carpool or ride the bus to work.

In addition to giving allowances, you will want to encourage your children to earn extra money on their own. You may choose to pay for extra chores. Even three or four year olds can fold clothes, empty the dishwasher, carry dishes from table to kitchen, and empty wastebaskets. You might pay a nickle for these jobs.

Five and six year olds can set tables, dust, vacuum, help put away dishes and groceries, take care of a pet, help clean the closets or bathroom, and straighten drawers. These might rate a dime.

Seven and eight year olds can empty the trash, sweep the patio and sidewalks, shovel snow, pack lunches, prepare cold meals, clean out the car, mop floors, or clean mirrors and low windows. You might pay ten cents a day for several of these tasks, or a quarter for some of the more difficult ones.

Children nine years old or older can do almost anything around the house if given appropriate instructions. You will want to pay them by the day or by the chore as warranted. For example, washing a car, cleaning out the refrigerator, mowing the lawn, painting, or ironing might rate one or two dollars.

What about collecting cans or newspapers? Or doing odd jobs for the neighbors? This method allows children to learn about job hunting. Spend an evening identifying the tasks your son is willing to do for pay. Discuss his qualifications and experience, and develop a brochure or flyer that will also serve as a mini-resume. Include references of people for whom your son has worked before. Type or neatly print the brochure and photocopy it. Next plan a marketing strategy. Will your child go door to door or just to specific neighbors you already know? How should your son dress before going out "job hunting"?

You and your son may be delightfully surprised at the results!

Teaching Practical Skills

The best way for our sons to learn how to maintain a home is to have chores to do as they grow up. The man who mixes colored clothes with the white ones in the washing machine probably never did the family laundry when he was a teenager. The one who can't sew on a button, cook an omelette, or paint a room probably didn't have many chores as he was growing up.

People learn best by doing, not by listening or watching, but by actually performing a task. I can take a course or read a book and learn about skiing, but I learn to ski by putting on my boots, stepping into the skis, and practicing skiing downhill. Your son will learn to do certain tasks by doing them. Therefore give him chores, not just to help you out around the house, but to prepare him to live on his own.

As soon as he is old enough, make him responsible for some of his own care and maintenance. He can do his own laundry and cook meals when you are not home. He can arrange for his own transportation some of the time and pay for his own long distance telephone calls. If you wait until your son is eighteen to say, "OK, you're totally on your own," the shock may be so great he can't face it and may attempt to stay in the nest longer. No longer caring for his every need is not a lack of caring, but a sign of real caring, because you are helping him develop independence and self-sufficiency.

A Spiritual Faith

To parents who have a strong personal faith in God, it is important that their children also accept that faith. Just as with the other values, first you tell, then you model. Let your children see you practicing what you believe. Talk openly about the Bible, your personal devotions, the sermon at church, and how your faith influences your decisions. Then be sure that you are not a "Sunday Christian" who behaves one way at church and another at home. When you fail to act consistently with your stated beliefs, try to acknowledge this to your son, and, if necessary, ask his forgiveness. In this area also, you will want to initiate discussions that will stimulate your son to consider spiritual values.

Young children may readily acknowledge and accept your faith, then during adolescence seem to question these beliefs. As hard as it is to accept the questioning, we must understand what is going on. We need not act as if a teenager who is allowed to question the reality of God will lose his faith. The sobering truth is that for many teenagers (and some adults) there has never been a transference of ownership of their faith. They have never moved from believing because someone said so to believing because they believe. Until this transference has occurred, the faith isn't really theirs to depend on.

Philip had been a Christian since he was ten. He knew all of the Bible stories and could quote over one hundred verses. He always won the Bible quiz contests in the youth group, but he had never owned his faith for himself. So when he went away to college and had several confrontations with an atheistic professor, he found himself unsure of what was true.

We see many illustrations of superimposed values in the home when children conform to the values and desires of their parents without adopting those values on a personal level. Therefore, in keeping with the methods we have been discussing for sharing values, you will want to encourage your sons to struggle with spiritual issues openly. You should be willing to discuss choices and consequences with them until they can truly come to an individual relationship with the Lord and a personal belief in the Bible as the Word of God and a valuable guide for life. Once they own that truth, their personal value systems will begin to conform to spiritual standards.

While there are many other values parents want to teach their children, almost everyone agrees that these four—honesty, caring, self-sufficiency, and a strong, spiritual faith—are the most critical.

Sometimes being a parent is a joy. Sometimes it hurts. But the important thing is to be committed to doing the best we can. We should recognize that even though our sons will choose their own values, if we use the three approaches in this chapter, we will probably find that we have had some influence on the values they chose.

Don't expect results overnight. You won't see them

that fast; but, if you are faithful, you will see hints of what your sons are becoming and of the positive values they are choosing. Those flashes of maturity are wonderfully encouraging to mothers raising sons alone.

I think that the principle of 1 Corinthians 3:6–8 applies to parenting. Paul is talking about how people receive the gospel. He says that sometimes one person plants the seed, another person waters, but it is God who gives the harvest. As a mother, I did my best to plant the right seeds. Others in my sons' lives have added to what I started, but I trust in God to bring my sons to the place where they will make the right choices and adopt the values He would have for them.

I can do no more. But He can.

Chapter

8

SEXUALITY
How Do I Teach My Son to be a Man?

I was cleaning closets in preparation for yet another move as a result of a job transfer when I found a crumpled letter. Scanning it to see if it was something to keep or toss, I saw it was addressed to my twelve-year-old son, dated two years earlier. It was from a girl and she was asking for nude photos from him in exchange for those she was enclosing of herself. She was offering to come over to our house one day after school for "a good time."

I was shocked, outraged, and a little curious. Just what had happened two years before when he had received that letter? (Nothing, according to my son.)

The whole area of sexuality is a difficult one for women raising sons alone. How do we as women teach our sons all they need to know about being a man?

As boys mature they develop an awareness of their own sexuality, and at the same time they also move from group relationships (relating to girls in a general way) to single relationships (forming friendships with girls on a one-to-one basis). We all have social needs for fellowship, conversation, working together, loving and being loved, sharing our feelings and having others share their feelings with us. In addition to these needs, teenage sons have special social needs. The development toward sexuality and the formation of single relationships result in their redefining their social interactions.

Sometimes a teen develops more in one of these areas than in another. Jim may be developing friendships with individual girls and guys but feels uncomfortable with his sexual feelings and urges, even to the point that he may not accept his own sexuality. Until he does, he won't be ready to give and take in a marriage relationship.

On the other hand, Bob may fully accept his sexuality (all of the feelings and emotions that are beginning to emerge) but not yet have developed the ability to relate to girls his own age. He may develop a crush on a female teacher because he sees in her qualities he considers ideal in a wife, and he has not seen these qualities in girls in his classes at school. Both Jim and Bob need further growth.

As our sons reach adolescence and begin to mature physically, we mothers face a new set of challenges in dealing with their budding sexuality. Looking back we realize that any embarrassment or difficulty we may have felt sharing the facts of sex with our sons when they were younger was easy compared to discussing the feelings and emotions of sexual relationships. Now we are anxious not only to share information but, at the same time, to pass on our values regarding chastity and morality. Our fears mount.

What if our sons become sexually active? What if they develop sexually transmitted diseases? What if they get girls pregnant? What if they don't like girls; what if they are gay? What if they get AIDS?

WILL MY SON BE GAY?

"My greatest fear as a single mom is that my son will become a homosexual," Ida admitted.

"Me, too!" Jean agreed. "I've always heard that the main cause of male homosexuality was having a strong mother and a weak father. So when there's no father around at all, wouldn't that increase the chances of my son being gay?"

Strong Mom, Absent Father

When encouraged to be open about what scares them most about being a single parent, many single moms around the country share similar fears. This is particularly true of those who have a strong Christian faith that includes the biblical perspective of homosexuality as unacceptable to God (Rom. 1:24–32; Lev. 18:22). In order to respond to these fears, I researched the subject. I talked to psychologists, gay men, and mothers of gay men; I read books and journals and talked to directors of Christian ministries to homosexuals who desire to come out of that lifestyle. I could find no significant correlation between being raised by a single mom and being gay.

The experts aren't in agreement about what causes male homosexuality, but several factors may play a part. A lack of bonding with a father (or father figure) in the first few years of life may cause a boy to grow up with a deep loneliness and desire for fatherly love and acceptance, so he may try to meet that need by seeking sexual attention from men. On the other hand, most men who grew up without a father in residence do not become gay.

Negative Experience with a Father or Father Figure

The absence of a father in residence is not the only reason the necessary bonding does not occur. "When my first husband died I was expecting our first son," Beverly recalled. "When my son was about eighteen months old I remarried, but I made the wrong choice. I came home from work early one day about six months later to find that my husband had stuffed my son into a chest and left him there all afternoon. When I angrily confronted my husband, he admitted that he had done the same thing every day for the last six months. I took my son and walked out.

"For the next several years I was very protective of my son, surrounding him with loving people, all women. I think that somewhere in his little mind, as early as two years old, he decided that women were good and kind and men were awful. He never wanted to be a man. Even though that early decision was buried in his subconscious, it influenced his development as he seemed to reject the more aggressive and power-related traits in his own personality in favor of allowing his tender and gentle side to be dominant. When he was twenty-three, he told me he was gay, and I was not surprised. I don't know if I could have changed my son's sexual orientation had I provided healthy male relationships in his life after his experiences with my ex-husband, but I was so shocked by his abusive behavior that I had a hard time trusting men for the next several years!"

Again, though, the majority of men whose fathers or stepfathers abuse them do not grow up to be gay.

However, all boys, not just those who have had bad experiences with a father or father figure, need a balance of relationships in their lives. As moms, we need to work at finding good relationships for our sons, especially when they are young. Our sons need role models who can help them develop an understanding of themselves as total, sexual beings. We can find such role models by requesting assignments to classes taught by men in public school or Sunday school, by hiring male sitters, involving them in activities that typically have male leadership (Boy Scouts, Little League and other team sports), finding a "Big Brother" (through the organization of that name, the church, or a friend), and, whenever possible, encouraging time spent with their father. I did all of these things because I was concerned about providing masculine influences in my sons' lives.

Clinging Mother

Ted's story illustrates how he believes his relationship with his mother influenced him to be gay. "Mom and Dad were divorced when I was seven, and I never saw my Dad again," he explained. "But Mom and I got along well by ourselves. We used to spend all of our free time together. I was like her special confidant. She encouraged me to learn to do the things she liked so we could do them together, since she had no close friends other than me. For years I didn't develop close friends either, because I had Mother."

This type of relationship can be frustrating for a boy

who has a serious need to please but who can never fulfill his mother's deeper needs for intimacy. His own sexual drives can be driven underground as he fails to develop normal relationships with friends of his own age.

"As I grew older," Ted continued, "I found I was not comfortable with girls my own age. And I preferred the quieter, more introverted boys as friends, even though I admired the forcefulness and power of the aggressive boys."

This conflict within Ted led him to experiment with homosexual activities, which he found physically stimulating and enjoyable without feeling that he was emotionally "betraying" his relationship with his mother. But even if Ted had grown up without going into the gay lifestyle, his relationship with his mother was unhealthy. Mothers must learn to take care of their own social needs without making their sons their all-in-all. They can take time to join singles groups that provide a variety of activities, take classes at the local community college, and develop a few close friendships. They must seek professional counseling if they are unable to risk reaching out to other adults.

Habit

"When I was about nine," Dennis shared, "a guy from school invited me to spend the night. That evening he asked me if I'd like to wrestle. I said sure. Then I found out that what he meant by wrestling was taking off our clothes, getting physically close, and fondling each other's genitals. It felt good! Several times that year my friend and I would get together and engage in similar sex play. The more we did, the more we enjoyed it. As I grew older I continued experimenting until I had my first real sexual experience at age sixteen. I never again looked at a girl with desire."

Habits can shape behavior. When the immediate consequences of an action are pleasurable, that action is reinforced and is likely to be repeated. A boy who experiences pleasure from sex play with a person of his own sex usually wants to repeat the experience again and again. Even though there is guilt and a sense that the action is wrong, if the relief and pleasure outweigh the guilt and shame, the boy may become hooked into a lifestyle pattern. On the other hand, there have been many boys who have willingly participated in homosexual activities with peers, or have been seduced by an older man to perform homosexual activities, who didn't grow up gay. Even some men who admitted that they experienced physical pleasure from those activities are totally heterosexual today.

Suggestions

What actually causes a boy to go into the gay lifestyle? I don't know. But while you may not have any influence over your son's sexual orientation, there are some things you can do to encourage the development of a healthy sense of sexuality.

1. Be comfortable with your own sexuality.

2. Provide several good male relationships for your son.

3. Develop a social network for yourself and encourage your son to have friends of both sexes.

4. Allow your son to develop his own personal blend of aggressive and passive characteristics. Encourage

his masculinity without making him the "man of the house."

5. Don't become so worried about his sexual orientation that you suspect he's gay just because he hasn't had a date with a girl by the time he is sixteen or so. Some boys grow up slower than others, that's all.

6. If your son does share with you that he is gay, and you are devastated, you may need to see a counselor to help you work through how to accept a person but reject his lifestyle. You will need to get past the heartbreak and get on with your own life.

7. If your son should develop AIDS, you may need to be the one who reaches out to him in love to do what you can to help.

WILL MY SON BE SEXUALLY ACTIVE?

The night before Norman was married he told his mother that he was glad he and Anna had waited until they were married to have sex. "There were times I didn't think we would make it," he confessed, "but, we're both excited about giving ourselves to each other and doing it right. We figured if you could abstain because you weren't married, we could too." His mom cried a few happy tears and breathed a deep sigh of relief.

Chastity has become increasingly rare in our world, although there has been a recent change in attitude because of fear of AIDS and other sexually transmitted, incurable diseases. Children are becoming sexually active at younger ages.

Sex is a reality we single mothers have to deal with. Most of us take our sexual values seriously and want our children to adopt the same values. Using the principles in the preceding chapter, we might then take the following steps to share our values with our sons.

1. Don't avoid all mention of sex. Share the facts of life at an appropriate early age. Two very helpful books are *Where Did I Come From?* and *Will I Like It?* both by Peter Mayle (Secaucus, NJ: Lyle Stuart, 1973). A good book for initiating a discussion on puberty is Peter Mayle's *What's Happening to Me?* (Secaucus, NJ: Lyle Stuart, 1975). A good book for initiating a discussion on sex is *Will I Like It?,* also by Peter Mayle. (NOTE: These books provide the biological facts; you provide the moral and spiritual guidelines.)

2. When providing the moral and spiritual input, use appropriate scripture verses, such as Hebrews 13:4; 1 Corinthians 5:9–13; 6:9–25; 7:1–5; Ephesians 5:3,5; 1 Thessalonians 4:3; and 1 Corinthians 10:13. Give good reasons for being chaste until marriage. Some of those are it is what God says we are to do; it is the right thing to do. There'll be no guilt over breaking God's laws, no fears of pregnancy or of acquiring sexually transmitted diseases, and no later comparison of one's spouse to former lovers. Self-control learned will be of help in possible future separations from one's spouse. It is a pleasure to be able to share sex first with one's mate.

3. Be a good model of your sexual values in your own dating life. Don't try to preach chastity from a lover's bed. Another way of modeling your value system is in formulating house rules. If you want your sons to be sexually pure, you will not watch or allow your sons to watch sexually explicit movies and television programs. In addition, you can prohibit bring-

ing home erotic magazines and books. And you can make bedrooms off-limits to visitors of the opposite sex.

4. Provide good reading material on the subject of sexuality for the boys. (Hint: Read the books yourself first.)

5. Initiate discussions where your son can begin to formulate a healthy value system for his sexuality.

Discuss television shows or movies and ask: How did being sexually active affect the character? What were the consequences? How realistic was the show? How did the character feel afterwards about his/her choices?

Talk about dating and ways dates can be kept at the friendship levels: Planning active rather than passive dates, such as hiking instead of sitting for hours in a darkened living room watching television; going out in groups or to group activities instead of always single dating; limiting time alone together; working on projects together.

Discuss the possible consequences and cost of premarital sex.

Pose situational questions for your son to respond to: What would you do if . . . ? How could you say no to . . . ? Suppose a girl . . . ?

Discuss the pressures on boys to be sexually active. In addition to peer pressure from other guys, many girls persistently pursue boys in attempts to initiate sexual activity.

Search scripture to learn what God says about sex.

6. If you discover that your son has become sexually active, you have some hard decisions to make. Jan's son was nineteen, and she demanded either that he

abstain from sexual activity or that he move out. He chose to move out. Karen's son was younger, though, and she struggled to enforce the standards she wanted him to follow. She believes she was successful. Sally found out the hard way that in her state, if a girl gets pregnant and the boy is still under eighteen, a parent (in this case, a single mother) may be legally held responsible for child support. She had to get a second job for two years to make the payments because her son wasn't working and couldn't make the child support payments.

LEARNING TO BE CARINGLY INTIMATE

We all know how to become physically intimate (touching, holding hands, kissing, hugging, fondling, and engaging in sexual intercourse), but not all of us have learned that there is a lot more we can do to become good friends, and truly intimate, with others. Jumping to the physical usually precludes exploration of the other levels of intimacy. God's ideal is for us to get to know one another before marriage and save the sexual expression of physical intimacy for after marriage. Encourage your son to learn how to be intimate in other ways during his dating days.

Intimacy comes in many forms as we relate to people on different levels: recreationally, socially, emotionally, intellectually, spiritually, and physically.

We can develop recreational intimacy by participating in sports, watching movies and television shows, playing table games, biking, hiking, roller skating, and any number of other activities. We get to know how the other person strategizes, thinks, responds to winning and losing, leads and follows, or is a member of a team. Very enlightening!

We can develop social intimacy by working on a community project, going to parties, talking on the telephone, participating in church groups and clubs, and going to the theatre or out to dinner. We learn the other's likes and dislikes, how well he/she can relate to others on a casual basis, and get a taste of his/her sense of humor.

We can develop emotional intimacy by sharing on a personal level, trusting, caring, investing in one another's lives, and making commitments to one another. We learn if the other can be trusted, the response to being loved, how love is shown. We see the results of feedback.

We develop intellectual intimacy as we discuss, debate, argue, exchange ideas, take classes, do research together, or share about books we like (or hate). We get an insight into how the other person thinks, reasons, conceptualizes, and stands politically. We come to know that person's value system.

We can become spiritually intimate as we attend church together, share about our beliefs, read the Bible together, work on church activities or projects together, pray together and discuss how our faith works for us.

A person who has developed these intimacy skills is more likely to be a kind and considerate lover when the time comes for physical intimacy. They are skills that will enrich your son's whole life.

The area of sexuality may be a challenge to you as a woman raising her sons alone, but you can help them to become sexually healthy men. Just remember that teaching sexual morals is just like teaching other values. Share with them your standards, show them the biblical principles in scripture. Model what you teach, and help them interact with a variety of choices in the field of sexuality. Encourage them to make the right choices and to feel good about having taken positive steps toward growing into mature, caring, and godly men.

Chapter
9

INDEPENDENCE
Will He Ever Grow Up?

Michael, my younger son, had moved out of my home when he was thirteen. He went to live with his father, ran away from there two years later, and, after a few months on his own, called me from another state to ask if he could come home to me. He said he had been living under a bridge in Phoenix and washing dishes in exchange for food. It broke my heart. Of course, I said he could come home. Within months he was rebelling against our house rules, such as no drugs and go to school. Once again he left, going to live with a family in the community. He got in trouble with the law and at sixteen was sent back to his father by the judge. Although his life turned around and he started working steadily, he didn't get along with his father and couldn't make it on his own, so once again he asked to come to live with me. I said yes, with conditions, this time. It was hard trying to readjust my life to having an eighteen year old in the house. He was too grown up to discipline and too immature to leave to his own choices. I found myself wondering, as I looked at his room and at the mess he left in the kitchen, if he would ever grow up! By growing up, I meant assuming responsibility and acting accordingly.

Today, almost three years later, Michael is showing signs of maturity. I'm beginning to believe that he is going to make it successfully, after all.

Other parents have the same feelings. Often, we can't wait until our sons do grow up.

"I'm counting the years until my job as a parent is finished," Eileen admitted. "My youngest son is fifteen. I'm doing the best I can at being a single mom, but seven years of juggling my schedule and energies to meet the demands of my job and my three sons has been more than enough already! I can't wait until they grow up and go out on their own!"

Billie agreed. "I'm not sure I'm really suited to being a mother, especially a single mom. When my husband died, I was left with two boys, ages ten and eight. It's been tough. The boys haven't made very good life choices. One's been in trouble with the law, the other has dropped out of school and lately has been experimenting with drugs. There are so many days when I just want to resign, but I don't know how. I'm counting the days until they are out on their own."

PLAN AHEAD FOR WHEN THE BOYS LEAVE HOME

Eileen and Billie do not expect to experience any emotional struggles over letting go of their children; they both look forward to it. But not all single parents feel that way. Custodial parents in particular often have a hard time relinquishing the children. A married mom has at least three basic roles: partner, parent, and person. A single mom has one less role to contend with and can devote more time and energy to being a parent and a person. However, in many cases both married and single moms devote a significant portion of their energies to the parenting role, giving only token recognition to the role of being a person. Consequently, when the children grow up and those mothers are relieved of the parenting role, some are not sure just who they are or what to do with their time. Since their schedules are no longer required to accommodate the demands or needs of children, new schedules must be developed to fit their changed needs.

Rose said, "If my husband were still alive, I think it would be easier. But my sons and I have become very close, and I'm going to hate to lose their companionship. They are all I have left. Today I still feel as if I have a family, but when the boys leave home, I'll be alone."

Daisy agreed. "Just when my son and I have finally developed a neat friendship, he's ready to go off to college. I'm going to miss him terribly."

Planning ahead can make the transition easier. Mable knows. "Early on I made sure that I had a little time each week just for me," explained Mable. "I needed quiet time to think, to work on a special project, and, later, to take a class that particularly interested me. When I first became a single parent, I had to really work at finding that extra little bit of time, but if I didn't I would start to get cranky and resentful of the children. So I just started putting *my time* on the schedule along with everything else that had to get done. When my sons left home, I discovered that I had plenty of things I wanted to do and had been saving until I had more free time. The transition was easy for me because I had planned for it. I miss the boys, of course, but I see them frequently and call them whenever I want to talk."

Here are ways you can plan ahead:

1. Train your children early to be independent and to handle responsibility so you won't feel as if you are carrying all of the responsibility and so you will have some free time. Feeling needed is great, but it can be addicting. Do things for your children because you want to, but don't make them totally dependent upon you.

One of your goals is to help your sons become dependent upon the Lord. Teach them to seek God's will, to search the scriptures for guidance, and to pray for wisdom. Both you and the boys need to claim Proverbs 3:5–6, which says that if we will trust in the Lord and acknowledge Him in all our ways that He will direct our paths. Boys need to trust the Lord, not trust in Mom!

2. Make the most of the years that you do have the children with you by scheduling quality time together. When choosing between a household chore and spending an hour sharing with your son because he wants to talk, choose the discussion. The housework can wait.

3. Develop your own interests, hobbies, talents, and abilities.

4. Have a dream list of things you would do if you were free to, or had a little more money in the family budget. Someday you will have both the extra time and money. Your list might include traveling, writing

a book, organizing the family photographs out of the shoebox and into albums, taking up photography, finding a new job, starting your own business.

5. Begin now to do what you can to prepare for the things on your list: Save a little money each month (twenty dollars a month over a five-year-period is twelve hundred dollars, not counting the interest); learn a foreign language; take classes.

Seeing our children go out on their own is sort of like graduation—for them and for us. If we truly believe that life is valuable and that each of us has a special plan for our lives (see Jer. 28:11; Rom. 12:1–2), then perhaps that time when our parenting commitment is over will be the start of something wonderful!

HELPING YOUR SON GROW TOWARD INDEPENDENCE

In order for your sons to become successful on their own, they must learn to cope with independence and exercise the appropriate level of self-discipline. Ideally, adolescent development leads from dependence to independence and from parental discipline to self-discipline.

We all begin life totally dependent on others for our basic physical needs: food, clothing, shelter, transportation, and discipline. While this is normal and acceptable in a young child, it is unacceptable in an adult. In our society, we expect well-balanced, mature adults to have developed the appropriate level of self-discipline for the amount of independence they exercise. However, one of the problems of growing up is that we do not usually grow toward responsible self-discipline and independence at the same rate.

Micky may be very self-disciplined and, consequently, very dependable when following instructions and keeping commitments, but may never have developed independence and therefore does not make his own decisions or use much initiative. On the other hand, Frank may be quite independent and capable of taking all kinds of risks, but if he has not learned self-discipline, he is actually reckless and irresponsible. Both Micky and Frank need further growth.

Often the most bitter arguments between single moms and their sons come when discussing which comes first, self-discipline or independence. The son's position is usually "Give me independence and I will develop responsibility." The mom's defense is "Show me responsibility and I will feel comfortable giving you more independence." These differing demands can become the basis of family tension and anxiety. The farther apart the expectations of the parent and the performance of the teen, the more tension can be predicted. Either the adult or the teen can reduce the tension by reducing her/his demands, but neither is usually willing to do so. The quickest way for a boy to gain independence is to become more self-disciplined, but that is easier said than done and does little to resolve an immediate crisis ("But I need the car *tonight!* How can I show you self-discipline right now?").

SELF-DISCIPLINE

The best definition I know for self-discipline is choosing to do what needs to be done instead of what one wants to do. It doesn't take self-discipline to do something we want to do, but when our wants differ from the right things to do, self-discipline is very necessary. This means that self-discipline is required in direct proportion to the number of choices one has to make.

Babies don't need self-discipline because they have very few choices. But as soon as they start to grow up they begin to have many choices. We first learn to make the right choices because we want to avoid making people unhappy with us, resulting in punishment. Later we learn to do or not do things in order to get what we want. We eat certain foods and decline others in order to lose weight. Or we decide not to buy on impulse in order to save money for a trip or a big purchase. We choose to spend time practicing the piano instead of watching television in order to be able to play music. As we develop in the area of self-discipline, we begin to make choices that are for the benefit of our community, so we obey traffic laws, respect the property and rights of others, and comply with the various rules and regulations that govern our lives.

As parents we need to work with our sons to assist them in the development of self-discipline. At first we set the house rules and make sure the children understand what is expected of them. When they fail to follow the rules, we must enforce the consequences consistently and fairly. But we also need to set up positive consequences to reward our sons for making good choices. Reinforcers might range from a hug and praise to special treats or being allowed to choose what to do on the next family night out.

Our sons need to learn self-discipline in order to function independently in life: to develop the skills they will need later in life; to decide what is most important, setting goals and working to achieve them; to hold their tongues at times when silence is the best option; to spend money on such boring things as fuel, food, utilities, and repairs instead of on prized possessions; to learn from their mistakes.

Self-discipline is the key to freedom, because as our sons demonstrate increased self-discipline, we trust them more and more to make their own choices. However, it seems hard for some kids to acknowledge the fact that with increased freedom comes more responsibility. With driving a car comes paying registration and insurance. With voting comes being asked to serve on juries. With a regular paycheck comes the need to be punctual and reliable on the job.

RESIST THE TEMPTATION
TO RESCUE YOUR SON
FROM POOR CHOICES

"My problem is that I tend to jump in and rescue my son from his poor choices," admitted Nell. "Like the last time he spent all of his allowance on a model airplane and didn't have enough left over to buy his lunch at school. He refused to carry a sack lunch, and I didn't want him to go hungry. So I gave him the extra money and a lecture on making wise choices."

Nell would have done better to skip the lecture and keep her money. Letting our children live with the consequences of making poor choices is often hard, but it is one of the best ways to help them learn self-discipline.

Unfortunately, many of us are rescuers. We don't want our sons to fail in school, so we take the responsibility for ensuring that homework is done long after our children are old enough to assume that responsibility. We don't want our sons to do without things that others have, so we provide beyond our means or we replace money that they have spent foolishly. We don't want them to miss out on attending an event so we drive them when they fail to make their own transportation arrangements as they promised to do when we agreed they could go.

Unless their health and safety are endangered we should let our sons learn from the natural consequences of their choices. That is hard to do. Many have been the nights I've gone to bed with an upset stomach because intellectually I knew I'd made the right decision, but emotionally I hurt to see my nineteen-year-old baby "suffering." But because I care and because I want him to mature, to develop self-control, wisdom, and self-discipline, I try to exercise self-discipline myself, doing what is right rather than what I really am tempted to do.

It is easier to do the right thing if we remember that God teaches us by letting us take the consequences of our actions. When we see that making wrong choices results in bad consequences, we usually decide not to make that same wrong choice again. Let God have the same freedom to teach your sons. Let Him work in their lives. Don't rescue.

TEACH YOUR SON HOUSEHOLD MAINTENANCE

One of the responsibilities independence eventually brings is taking care of a home of one's own. You can help prepare your sons for living on their own by ensuring that they know how to do the basic chores. In some ways your boys have an edge over others, because they are often forced to grow up a little faster than if there were two adults in the home. They will most likely be expected to assist in the management of the family.

As long as you do not become overly dependent upon your sons to the extent of robbing them of their childhoods or form unhealthy emotional attachments with them, the increased responsibility can be good for them. Boys who have more responsibility also tend to have more freedom because they have developed self-discipline at a younger age. The relationship between the parent and the child is more of a *partnership* than a *power trip*. The letting-go process as boys become young adults is easier on both the parent and the children. Boys can grow up with positive self-images because they know they can handle adult responsibilities. Those who have been exposed to the realities of and responsibilities for some of the tasks involved in managing a home are better equipped to run their own households when they move out of the parental home.

Thus if you ever feel guilty about asking your sons to help out around the home, consider these positive outcomes. Get them involved. It is their home too!

THE CLIMB TO INDEPENDENCE IS UPHILL

Joan shared, "When I get really angry with my son for not growing up as fast as I think he should, I stop and take a look at myself. Some days I wish I had someone to take care of me, to pick up after me, to pay my way for me, and to rescue me from the consequences of poor choices. On those days, I'm not much different from my son."

The journey from dependence to independence is an uphill struggle. There are times our sons will take one step backward for every two steps they take forward. But if you can pull back from the immediate conflict to get a broader perspective, you will usually find that overall there has been progress.

Chapter

10

ENCOURAGEMENTS
Sometimes I Want to Resign!

Radios. Records. Hiking boots. Electronic games. Coats.

Up and down the department store aisles I strolled trying to find the right Christmas gifts for my sons. What could I give them that they would like and that would adequately convey my message of love? Somehow The Perfect Gift didn't leap out at me from any of the displays.

"It's the thought that counts," I muttered to myself, grabbing a couple of items and hurrying to the checkout counter. The long line scarcely moved. Fifteen minutes later I was still in line, with several people ahead of me. As I looked at what I was holding I realized that these were not the right gifts, so I returned the items to the shelf, left the store, and drove home.

Christmas morning the boys opened all of their gifts from friends and relatives before discovering the envelopes I had hidden for last. "Money!" they shrieked enthusiastically. "That's the best gift of all. It's just what we wanted!"

And it was, but it wasn't what I had wanted to give them. They were pleased, but I felt slightly depressed. I thought of how often we parents want to give our children not just the basic necessities of life, or even possessions, but something more, and of how often the children end up receiving something less. We want to give all of our values, and they are only interested in a few. We want to give them independence and they cling to dependency in certain areas. We try to give them self-esteem and a positive self-image and still they experience doubts and insecurities. But we must continue to try to give good gifts to our sons.

Throughout this book, I've dealt with several gifts we try to pass on to our sons. Let's review these in a quick summary.

LOVE

Because we want to give our children the gift of love, we get up early or stay up late working to provide income and complete the chores. We worry about, fuss over, and nag them about homework. We hope that they will see through our tiredness and shortcomings and know that we truly love them.

Sometimes we forget that love is communicated best in other ways. We can show our son love whenever we stop what we are doing and listen to what he wants to say. We can show love when we ask for and respect his ideas and opinions, when we include him in the planning phase of chores or leisure-time activities, when we are affectionate, when we ask forgiveness for our own mistakes and allow him to make a few of his own.

Communicating love this way not only gives love but also builds self-esteem and confidence.

SELF-DISCIPLINE

Harold dropped into one of the large overstuffed chairs in the family room and sighed happily. "I'm tired!" he announced. As he proceeded to list all of the chores he had set for himself and completed that day, his mom, Irene, secretly smiled to herself. Was it possible that finally, at age seventeen, Harold was learning to discipline his own time, to put responsibility before fun? There had been so many times when she had been sure this day would never come.

It will not always be easy for you to separate nagging and supportive reminding or to let your sons take the natural consequences of their own lack of discipline. Nevertheless since you want them to be able to stand on their own when they leave home, you must resist the temptation to rescue them from their own failures.

ASSERTIVENESS

Helen and Dan were arguing. Dan wanted to borrow a hundred dollars to go on a trip with a friend. Helen was refusing to give her eighteen-year-old son the money. As the argument proceeded, tempers flared and Helen lashed out, "You would have the money yourself, if you wouldn't take time off from work for no reason at all like you did today! If you need money, go to work like the rest of us. If you don't watch out and keep on making stupid choices like that, you're going to end up broke and unemployed, just like your father!"

Dan, who had been ready to hurl a matching retort, stopped and quietly said, "Mom, I don't like it when you put me down. I was sick today and didn't feel like working. I don't want you to put me down. If you won't give me the money, okay, but don't put me down!"

Helen's mouth nearly dropped open. The argument was over and the money was forgotten in her pleased surprise at the assertiveness of her son. How great that he was learning to express his feelings and ask for what he wanted in relationships!

We usually want our sons to learn assertive techniques, but sometimes, unlike Helen, we aren't willing for those techniques to be used with us. That's the price of open communication. Helen was pleased because Dan's style when growing up had been much more closed, moody, and passive-aggressive.

You will want to watch for and affirm signs of assertiveness in your son.

RELATIONAL SKILLS

"I want my son to grow up and be able to have good relationships, both friendships and romances, " Georgia stated. "It's hard to try to teach about relationships when I'm still learning myself."

Relational skills can be difficult to define because each relationship has its own types of interactions and styles. You can model and encourage your sons to practice being open, honest, caring, and forgiving. You can help them learn ways to express strong emotions (even negative ones) in an acceptable, even productive manner. Then you will most likely be successful in passing on this gift to your sons.

Most importantly, we want to give our sons good memories of their lives with us so they will know that family living can be fun and harmonious. I gave them memories, all right:

There was the time I took them to Mexico, and we were kidnapped! (Some American tourists aggressively sought—took!—our help to rescue their car.)

The time we went for a three-day cruise, it was foggy and cold the entire time, so we were cooped up inside. ("Mom, there isn't anything interesting to do!" they wailed for three days.)

I tried so hard and failed so often! But guess what the kids' favorite memories are?

The time the electricity failed, and we had to light candles and camp out in the living room, roasting hot dogs over the fire in the fireplace.

The time it rained so hard the streets were flooded, and we had to wade out to the car, splashing through the water in our boots.

The time we spent an entire weekend playing a marathon Monopoly game, stopping only to sleep and grab snacks.

All the spontaneous, out-of-the ordinary times and events that we enjoyed together, that's what they remember fondly.

So much of the time we try too hard to entertain our children, ending up with none of us having much fun because something always seems to go wrong with our *big* plans. Thus when we have invested a great deal in making something really special happen, we are disappointed if it isn't perfect.

You can give your sons good memories of growing up in a single parent family:

- Learn what your sons enjoy doing and share that with them.
- Decide as a family what project or sport would make a good family activity and do that.
- Make your home a place where the boys' friends are welcome and come to have fun.
- Encourage your boys to be open about their ideas, thoughts, feelings, and dreams.
- Give the boys things you make yourself: cookies, beanbags, pillows, bathrobes, cards.
- Watch some of the boys' favorite television shows with them.
- Spend evenings retelling little anecdotes from when the boys were little.
- Take time to enjoy life yourself. Give yourself a few good memories along the way, too.

Self-esteem

So many boys either never develop or during adolescence lose a healthy sense of self-esteem. Often our attempts to build that esteem into their lives seem to fail. We brag about or remind them of past accomplishments, compliment their appearance, deny their feelings of inadequacy ("You are *not* stupid!"). Yet we fail in this area because we do not recognize that esteem is a *self*-concept. It is not our opinion of the children that counts most but their own opinion of themselves.

Another way we can give the gift of self-esteem is by discovering what skills, knowledge, accomplishments, or characteristics the children want to master/acquire and assist them to set and achieve goals in these areas. We can facilitate that process by suggesting how the goals can be divided into small, reachable steps, in brainstorming alternative ways to reach those steps, and affirming each sign of progress. As our children discover that they can become the persons they want to be, their self-confidence and self-esteem grow.

Values

In addition to the other values we want to pass on to our sons, we usually want to share our spiritual faith with them.

"Go to Sunday school and church. Read your Bible. Memorize scripture. Pray," we tell our children, hoping they will develop a personal relationship with God. Those admonitions are certainly important in the process. Faith in God is a gift from Him (Eph. 2:8–9) and comes from reading and hearing the Word of God (Rom. 10:17).

But our sons will be influenced by their observations of how faith works in our own life. As we walk according to our beliefs, we provide examples of how our faith sustains us through troubled times.

Whether or not our sons choose any of the values that we want for them, we must learn to express love and acceptance for who they are, in spite of their practices.

Sexuality

We want to give our sons the gift of being comfortable with their sexuality. This means that first we must be comfortable with our own. Open communication from an early age is the best way to start, but if it is too late for that, then start now. At first there may be some awkwardness if sexuality is not a subject you are used to discussing, but the more conversations you have, the easier it gets. Besides, how are you going to attempt to pass on your values in this area without some discussion?

Independence

Twenty-nine-year-old Wally has just moved back in with his mom for the third time. Mom is getting tired. "When is he going to grow up?" she wonders.

It's understandable why sons tend to stay at home longer than daughters do. Women are trained to run their own homes, but many men were either never taught or have never acknowledged that they need to take care of themselves. Who wouldn't want a mom to pick up after them, cook for them, and run their daily errands? But there is a time to grow up.

There are several aspects to being independent: financial, homemaking, decision making, emotional. If our sons are to learn independence in each of these areas, we must start early to let go.

I think that some of the clinging to dependence occurs because of us mothers who secretly miss that wonderful feeling of being needed when we first brought home a newborn from the hospital. Not only do our sons cling, but so do we.

We must let go. We must continue to love, but the strings must be cut.

YOU WILL NEED TO HANG TOUGH SOMETIMES

The process of training up children in the way they should go is tough. There are so many times when mothers want to resign, to quit, to give up. A lot of single parents I share with have one complaint in common: "I didn't sign on for this!" they exclaim. Few of us fantasized ourselves as single parents during our growing-up years.

Parenting isn't all that it is cracked up to be. One of the current books on parenting claims that babies have the best press in the world, and that's true. Who can resist a sweet, tiny baby all wrapped in a fuzzy blanket? But babies grow up, we discover, and the process of growing up is a very long one. Often moms find themselves thinking, "Wait a minute! Where does it say that just because I have a son that I also have to raise him alone, contend with his teachers, listen to the neighbor's complaints, handle all of the crises . . ."

There's Just Too Much to Do

Do you start each day with a list of things to do and find that regardless of how hard you work you never seem to finish? So you add the leftover items to the next day's list, which also never gets done?

A sense of being overloaded is common in a single parent home because one adult is trying to do all of the tasks of home maintenance, which is at the very least a two-person job. It can be done, of course, but the cost may be too high. Whenever one person attempts to do a two-person job for a sustained period of time, the results are fatigue, tension problems, high blood pressure, irritability, lack of energy, a diminished capacity to perform in all areas, and a loss of self-esteem. It is often better to decide what is reasonable for one person to do and then try to attack only those duties. Helpful hints for smart moms include:

- List all the tasks you have to do.
- Rate each as "must do," "should do," "would do if there were time."
- Prioritize the "must do" list.
- Focus only on the top priorities from this list.
- Find time for some of the "should do's" and "would do's" by delegating tasks to the children, reducing the frequency of some tasks, combining some tasks, and learning shortcuts.

Of course, sometimes you will wish that you had done everything on all three of your lists, but most of the time you will be glad that you have made time to be a person instead of a slave. Persons make better parents than do slaves or robots.

Coping with Stress

"I feel stretched to my limits. I can't take another problem with the children!" Sharon sighed wearily at the end of a horrible week.

At one time or another we each experience symptoms of stress overload, caused by having to cope with too many changes, problems, or demands within a short period of time, or by having a few severe stressors continue for too long a period of time. Since we live in a world of accelerating progress and changes, we are all subject to increased opportunities for stress overload.

A certain amount of stress is good for us because it provides the push needed to overcome inertia. However, too much stress is dangerous and can cause *distress*. People experience stress overload when they no longer maintain balance in their lives. When this overload occurs, energy is diverted from various areas in the body to support the stress response. If the situation is short-lived, the body quickly returns to homeostasis or equilibrium. On the other hand, if the stress is prolonged, sufficient energy to maintain a healthy body is no longer available and illness may occur.

People tend to live to the limits of their resources. We spend all of our incomes. We schedule all of our time so that we can't accommodate unexpected delays or demands very easily. Often we accept more stressors (demands) than we can handle with our reserve energies, so when we encounter unexpected stressors, we are unable to cope effectively because we have no extra energy.

We need time to learn stress management skills. Just as stress overload builds up over a period of weeks, perhaps even years, we learn to take control of the internal responses to external demands over a period of time.

The following list offers some steps to help with stress management.

- Keep a written record of things that cause you stress. Try to eliminate as many as you reasonably and practicably can.
- Set priorities, then devote your energies to those top priorities in your life.

- Live consistently with your beliefs so as to eliminate inner tension.
- Learn specific interventions for coping with those things that cause you the most stress and that you cannot eliminate from your life.
- Set up a reward system for yourself when you are functioning well and coping with life in the midst of stress.
- Follow the rules for good health: get enough sleep and rest, eat a balanced diet, exercise, maintain a balanced schedule, talk out negative feelings, have regular medical checkups, and avoid self-medication.
- Take frequent breaks during periods of high stress.
- Learn to physically relax.
- Use biofeedback.
- Take classes in stress management.
- Engage in a highly reinforcing activity upon arriving home from work.
- Limit the amount of work you bring home from the office.
- Learn to make decisions and then not to worry about whether or not you made the best decision.
- Obtain closure on unfinished tasks, relationships, and situations in your life.
- Be assertive.
- Practice acceptance and forgiveness.

Trying to be a supermom is unreasonable. Do your best, and accept not only your own limits but those of others. It is possible to live with stress—without distress.

When the going gets tough, hang tough. You can make it through.

YOU'LL ALSO NEED TO HANG LOOSE AT TIMES!

Hawaiians have a hand signal by which a fist is made with the three middle fingers while the thumb and little finger stick out. Waved about, this means Hang loose! Be cool! Relax! The message is Don't try *too* hard.

Do you ever feel as if you are trying so hard but getting nowhere? Trying too hard to ensure that your sons are happy and enjoying themselves is a common mistake single moms make.

When I took my two boys camping for the weekend, I packed the frisbee, the battery-operated television, food, and swimsuits. For two days the boys argued, refused to participate in any of the activities offered by the campground, enjoyed nothing I had planned, and complained of being bored.

Earlene planned a "See America" car trip for her teenagers one summer. All she heard was, "How many more days before we get home, Mom?"

Carla insisted that her boys participate in Little League baseball. Every other day, they argue about going to practice, ending up angry with one another.

Most of us have had the experience at least once of having our perfectly designed plans for the family fall apart because our needs, desires, or preferences don't match those of our sons, or because we miscalculated when we planned what we thought would interest them. This can be particularly frustrating when the arrangements were complicated and expensive and other people were also involved. Perhaps there is a better way.

We must remember that we cannot force our children to be happy or enjoy something. It is usually best to involve the boys in what we are planning for family activities rather than to spring a surprise on them, because the surprise may be ours instead, when the whole experience turns out to be a flop. We must not try too hard to do it all. It is not always the big things that make children remember family times with nostalgia.

When I was first divorced, I lived in a low-income housing apartment complex and my sons were in a child care center there. It wasn't a very good one because at five o'clock they simply closed and sent the children home. If I could have afforded a better option, I would have found one, but since I got off work at 4:15 and only worked six miles away, I didn't foresee a problem. Each day I rushed home and was almost always there by 4:35. Then one day it rained and there was an accident on the freeway that tied up traffic for two hours. While I sat in my car, frustrated and angry, I imagined my two little boys being sent home alone. It was getting dark, and it was cold and rainy outside. I felt sick at my stomach and helpless to do anything about getting home any sooner. Finally the accident was cleared and we were allowed to proceed. I hurried home and my worst fears were realized. There on the step sat the boys, huddling together, scared, and soaking wet. They had obviously been wading in the five or six inches of water along the curb.

Feeling awful, I hurriedly bundled them inside, gave them warm baths, prepared their favorite supper, and cuddled and coddled them all evening. In fact, I spent the next several weeks making it up to them. Also, I immediately found a different child care center. For a long time I felt like a failure as a mother for having put my children through such an ordeal.

Guess what Michael's favorite story was as he grew up? The big flood in Sacramento when he and Jon had to swim home and Mom couldn't get home all night! Today's disasters may turn out to be tomorrow's favorite stories.

I asked several adults who grew up in single parent homes what made it good for them and came up with the following three attitudes.

1. Mom's attitude toward our situation

If you are angry, frustrated, resentful, bitter, or unhappy about being a single parent, you will pass on those attitudes and feelings to your sons. Your boys will grow up feeling deprived, cheated, and angry toward one or both of their parents.

In contrast, if you face reality with a possibility-thinking attitude you communicate the positive side of life to your sons. Even children who grew up in homes that never had enough money, let alone any luxuries, did not always feel that they had been "poor." Their perceptions usually depended on the attitude and atmosphere created by the mother.

2. Mom's relationship with us

"Mom used to play games with us in the evenings," Joel remembered.

"Mom used to trust me as if I were grown up," Artie said.

If you take time to be with your sons, sharing together, laughing and having fun as a family, as well as talking through serious subjects, your boys will grow up feeling good about their childhoods. If you are too busy working, working, working, to ever have time for the boys, they will grow up feeling that they were deprived.

3. Mom's attitude toward Dad

The lack of a good relationship with the absent parent seems to leave the deepest scars on children from single parent families. Whether this lack is due to death or divorce, the pain feels like rejection and the loss of a beautiful "what might have been." If the other parent is alive, there is usually a natural curiosity to get to know him. The mother's attitude toward the father and his relationship with the boys will often color their perceptions of the growing-up years. "Mom never minded when I called or visited my dad," David said. "I could see him as much as I wanted. Some of my friends used to have to sneak around to meet their fathers or call them from a friend's house. But not me. Even though my folks were divorced, I still grew up with two parents. We didn't have any big problems."

An ideal family? No, just a single mom with the right attitude.

IT IS YOUR LIFE!

Do you ever feel you aren't getting from life all that you had hoped for? If you do, then stop right now and decide to take charge of your life:

1. Determine where you are now and where you want to be.

2. Recognize that the difference between what you are and what you will become is what you do.

3. Accept the realities in your life that cannot be changed, such as your height, age, single state (at this time, at least).

4. Identify what can be changed.

5. Identify what *you will change*. Write realistic, measurable, and dated goals.

6. Implement your action plan and evaluate your progress.

Doing a self-assessment every few months is an important part of growing. In this way you will know where you've been, where you are going, and how far along you are. The abundant life can be yours. If you aren't one of those people who are enjoying the adventure of being a single mom, make some changes.

It is your life! Make it worth living!

Jesus said in John 10:10 that He came that we might have an abundant life. Go for it!

Appendix A
Helpful Promises from Scripture

Often participants in my single parent discussion groups share favorite Bible verses they've found to be especially helpful during tough parenting times. Here is their list to help you through your tough times:

When You Need Help

Deuteronomy 10:18	God promises to provide justice, food, and raiment to the fatherless.
Deuteronomy 14:29	God promises sufficient food for the fatherless.
Job 29:12	God promises to deliver the fatherless.
Psalm 10:14	God promises to help the fatherless.
Psalm 33:20	God is your help.
Psalm 37:40	God will help you in times of trouble.

Psalm 40:17	God knows you and will help you.
Psalm 46:1	God is a very present help in trouble.
Psalm 68:5	God promises to be a father to the father-less.

When You Don't Feel Smart Enough

Proverbs 2:6–7	God stores up wisdom for you.
Proverbs 3:5–6	God will direct your path.
Proverbs 4:5–6	You should get wisdom from God.
James 1:5	You can ask for and receive wisdom from God.

When You Can't Take Any More

Psalm 18:32	God girds you with strength.
Psalm 19:14	
Psalm 29:11	
Ephesians 3:16–20	God will strengthen your inner self.
Philippians 4:7	God will keep your heart and mind.

When You Are Unhappy and Upset

Psalm 16:11	There is joy in the presence of God.
Psalm 51:8	God gives joy.
Isaiah 26:3	God will give you peace.

John 15:9–10	Christ wants your joy to be full.
John 15:11	Christ's joy will remain in you.
John 16:22	No one can steal away your joy.
Galatians 5:22–23	Joy and peace are yours through the Spirit.
Philippians 4:6–9	You can have peace.
Colossians 3:15	God will give you peace.

When You Feel Your Efforts Are in Vain

Psalm 30:5	Your weeping won't last forever.
Psalm 126:5	Joy will follow your tears.
Proverbs 22:6	If you train your children in the way they should go, even if you don't see signs now, they will not depart from it when they grow up.
Proverbs 23:24	You will rejoice when your children show wisdom.
Galatians 6:7–9	You will reap if you are faithful.

When You Have Your Own Needs

| Isaiah 54:5 | God tells Israel that He is her husband (a |

promise I claimed
when I felt I needed a
man to turn to, a
spouse to help me
with the parenting
task).

Matthew 21:22 John 15:1-7	God will answer your prayers.
John 14:13–14	Ask God for help.
Philippians 4:19	God will supply your needs.
1 John 5:14–15	Ask God believingly and He will answer.

When You Have Failed

Joshua 1:8–9	You can be successful if you make the right choices.
Psalm 37:4–5	If you trust Him, He will work things out.
Colossians 1:14; 2:13 Ephesians 1:7 James 5:15 1 John 1:9	God will forgive you.
Ephesians 1:6	You are accepted in Christ.

Appendix B
Single Parenting Discussion Starters

You will find it very helpful to get together with other single moms to talk about your experiences. If the informal structure doesn't work, divide the group into clusters of three or four people and have each person respond to five or six of the following questions or incomplete statements. This should spark enough discussion to last an hour.

1. Single parenting means . . .
2. The differences between a widowed single parent and a divorced one are . . .
3. Being a single parent is easier (or harder) than being a married parent because . . .
4. Describe the typical single mom with custody of her sons.
5. List the challenges of being a single mom.
6. What things do never-married mothers have in common with single-again mothers?

7. Define "shared custody" and tell how it works.

8. I think that shared custody is good/bad because . . .

9. I think that men/women are better prepared to be parents because . . .

10. One way in which I was unprepared for parenting was . . .

11. My former spouse is still very much a part of my children's lives because . . .

12. My family's response to my role of being a single parent has been . . .

13. My friends are most helpful when . . .

14. One way my friends and I have made parenting easier for one another is . . .

15. My experiences with single parent organizations have been . . .

16. The church has helped me as a single parent by . . .

17. I depend on God the most as my co-parent when . . .

18. My most embarrassing moment as a single mom was when . . .

19. My biggest problem/joy with being a single parent is . . .

20. I find that people respond to my being a single mom by . . .

21. A problem with single parenting I overcame was . . .

22. A funny experience I had as a single mom was . . .

23. Sometimes I feel like . . .

24. I almost give up when . . .

25. The rewards of being a single parent include . . .

26. An experience I remember because it was so good was when . . .

27. Sometimes I tell God that . . .

28. Single parenting is better than . . .

29. I feel good about myself as a parent when . . .

30. I experience a sense of responsibility overload when . . .

31. When I feel overloaded, I . . .

32. I feel emotionally overloaded when . . .

33. One way I reduce my overload is . . .

34. Now that I am single again, my son and I . . .

35. The biggest problem with my budget is . . .

36. I make financial ends meet by . . .

37. I learned to live within my budget when . . .

38. I have found I am refreshed and ready to tackle being a parent after I . . .

39. Through my single parenting experience, I have learned . . .

40. I have provided role models of the opposite sex for my sons by . . .

41. I have resolved my child care problems by . . .

42. The hardest thing about arranging child care is . . .

43. My son's relationship with (or memory of) his dad is easy/hard for me because . . .

44. My biggest fear as a single mom is . . .

45. I wish I were wiser when it comes to . . .

46. One thing I handled well even though I was afraid was . . .

47. I feel weak and helpless when . . .

48. I depend on God's strength when . . .

49. The pressure I find most difficult to handle is . . .

50. I think that being a noncustodial parent is hard because . . .

51. People sometimes think that noncustodial parents . . .

52. I am most lonely when . . .

53. Loneliness is my friend because . . .

54. One way I set myself up for being lonely is . . .

55. I have found that I can overcome my feelings of loneliness if I . . .

56. I am most afraid of being replaced in my son's affections when . . .

57. My relationship with my son has improved now that I am single, because . . .

58. When I miss my son, I . . .

59. When I became single the house rules I changed were . . .

60. My son's role as a family member has changed in that . . .

61. I depend on my son for . . .

62. I expect my son to . . .

63. I relate to God as a friend when . . .

64. I consider God my heavenly parent when . . .

65. The thing I pray for most frequently is . . .

66. I have discovered that my expectations for myself as a single mom are . . .

67. Examples of self-expectations I have modified to be more realistic are . . .

68. I handle the "income production" tasks at our home by . . .

69. The home maintenance jobs at our home are handled by . . .

70. Some of the creative ways I have squeezed out free time for myself are . . .

71. I have reduced unnecessary conflicts in our family by . . .

72. When people criticize me, I . . .

73. The key to coping with criticism is . . .

74. In order to benefit from criticism I have found that I . . .

75. My supportive network includes . . .

76. I turn to my support when . . .

77. I have built affirmation into my life by . . .

78. When I feel depressed, I . . .

79. My experiences with reaching out to people have been good/bad because . . .

80. The ways I try to avoid being rejected when I do reach out include . . .

81. The way I feel when I am rejected is . . .

82. My normal response to rejection is . . .

83. I have learned to handle rejection by . . .

84. An example of a negative attitude that I have reprogrammed into a positive viewpoint is . . .

85-100. Here is a list of negative attitudes. How could they be reprogrammed into positive statements? For example: "I am lonely" can be reprogrammed to "I feel alone and need affirmation. I will call a friend."

   85. I am a failure.
   86. I am all alone.
   87. No one loves me.
   88. I hate Friday nights when I don't have a date.
   89. I am too busy to make friends.
   90. I have no friends.
   91. I can't do everything I am expected to do.
   92. I can't have a lasting relationship.
   93. My children don't want me to date.
   94. I can't go out and leave the kids at home.
   95. I hate being a single parent.
   96. I never have any time for myself.
   97. I never have any fun.
   98. Life is a drag.
   99. I am too old to start over.
   100. I don't want to be a single parent.

101. A very helpful class I attended on single parenting was . . .

102. The church can help single moms by . .

103. Dating the second time around has been . . .

104. What I miss most about being married is . . .

105. Dating today is different than it was when I was a teen, because . . .

106. If a genie appeared before you and offered to fulfill three wishes, what would you ask for? Explain your choices.

107. If God gave you the same option, what would you ask for?

108. Were your two sets of wishes the same? If not, why not?

109. Letting go of the past is hard/easy because . . .

110. I have learned to forgive my past by . . .

111. When I have a big problem and need help in resolving it, I . . .

112. Community resources I have found helpful as a single mom are . . .

113. Ways single moms have to let go of their sons include . . .

114. Letting go of the children is hard/easy because . . .

115. When I "grow up" I want to be . . .

116. What part does goal setting play in your life?

117. Which goals are the hardest for you to reach?

118. Share a goal you set and achieved that meant a lot to you.

119. List one strength you have in each of these areas: physical, emotional, spiritual, intellectual, social.

120. Share one thing you have always wanted to do but never tried.

121. The parenting skill I am most accomplished at is . . .

122. The parenting skill I need more practice with is . . .

123. My children think that as a mom I . . .

124. I feel I have failed when . . .

125. I know I am a success when . . .

Appendix C
Resources for Single Mothers

OTHER BOOKS BY BOBBIE REED

I Didn't Plan to Be a Single Parent, St. Louis, MO:
Concordia Publishing House, 1981.

Based not only on my own experiences as a single
mother, but also on hundreds of hours of discussion
with single mothers and their children; interviews
with pastors, Christian educators, marriage, family,
and child counselors, psychologists and attorneys who
handle divorce and custody cases, this book offers
sympathetic and practical suggestions on handling
such issues as

- Evaluating expectations
- Redefining roles, rules, and responsibilities
- Developing a supportive network
- Dating the second time around
- Resolving legal issues
- Letting the children go.

Stepfamilies—Living in Christian Harmony, St. Louis, MO: Concordia Publishing House, 1980.

If you are considering remarriage, you will become a stepfamily. If your ex-spouse has remarried, your children are already a part of a stepfamily. This book discusses dealing with the new stepparent in your sons' lives, resolving legal leftovers, and understanding the special and unique challenges that face members of a stepfamily.

Contrary to glowing expectations and bright hopes, the everyday realities of steprelationships are often harsh. Yet stepfamilies can be successful if each member recognizes that relationships are fragile and need to be handled with prayer.

Christian Family Activities for One Parent Families, Cincinnati, OH: Standard Publishing, 1982.

This provides a year's worth of ideas for a weekly family night. Fifty-three different topics of interest to single-parent families are presented. Each week's ideas include discussion starters, fun activities, and a suggestion for opening God's Word to see what He has to say about the topic. Sample topics include:

- What is different now?
- What I miss most
- Feeling safe
- Surviving a divorce
- Coping with death
- The parent I live with most
- My other parent
- Who takes out the trash?

Too Close, Too Soon, with Jim Talley, Nashville, TN: Thomas Nelson Publishers, 1982.

Avoiding the pitfalls in romantic relationships is a challenge not only for teenagers but also for single mothers. As you succeed in modeling the Christian ideals in your relationships, you can become an effective guide for your sons. It is hard in today's fast-paced social environment to be prepared to withstand pressures for instant gratification. Distorting the need to love and be loved into brief sexual flings, some singles suffer emotionally destructive side effects: loneliness, rejection, guilt, and feelings of having been used. This book provides practical ways to build good relationships between men and women without premature sexual intimacy.

NEWSLETTER

Dads and Moms (quarterly) and *Dads Only* (monthly), P.O. Box 340, Julian, CA 92036.

This excellent newsletter is packed with short, practical ideas for parenting. Don't let the title keep you from checking it out. Ideas include holiday theme activities, communication hints, and new resources for parents. Write for a sample copy. Better yet, subscribe!

CURRICULUM

God can help my owies (ages 2–6) and *God can heal my hurts* (ages 7–12), by Jim and Barbara Dycus, 1199 Clay Street, Winter Park, FL 1986.

Jim and Barbara have written some wonderful curricula for use in groups, should you be looking for something to help in working with children of divorced parents. Complete with teacher's manuals, these focus on helping children begin their journey into recovery and coping with the common emotions of grief, guilt, rejection, anger, depression, and a loss of self-esteem. They also guide the children toward growth in starting over, building new relationships, and gaining independence.

BOOKS

There are many books being written every year for single parents. Here are some I think are particularly good:

Gardner, Richard, *The Boys and Girls Book About Divorce,* New York: Bantam Books, 1971.

Gardner, Richard, *The Boys and Girls Book About One Parent Families,* New York: Putnam, 1978.

In both of these books Richard Gardner communicates to teenagers at their level about the painful topics of divorce and living in a single parent home. He raises hard-to-talk-about subjects and gives simple, pragmatic perspectives that youngsters can find comforting.

Gordon, Thomas, *Parent Effectiveness Training,* New York: Wyden, 1976.

Gaulke, Earl H., *You Can Have a Family Where Everybody Wins,* St. Louis, MO: Concordia Publishing House, 1975.

Thomas Gordon's book provides options to parenting by power struggles and communicating by edict. He shows the fallacy of trying to win by intimidating children into obedience. Following his techniques can change the parenting experience from frustrating to exciting as children develop skills they will need to function successfully in today's world.

Earl Gaulke's book is a companion book to Thomas's and provides the biblical perspective for the techniques recommended by Thomas. Both are great guidebooks.

Lewis, Margie M. *The Hurting Parent,* Grand Rapids, MI: Zondervan, 1980.

When you feel as if you are hurting badly and no one understands just what you are going through, try reading this book. You will find that you are not alone, and that others have felt as frustrated, hurt, alone, and defeated as you. They have made it through. You can too!

Kesler, Jay, *Too Big to Spank,* Ventura, CA: Regal Books, 1978.

What do you do when your son gets too big to spank, yet refuses to listen to you? Tackle him in the front yard? Call the police and confess to inadequacy? Have a breakdown? Run away?

Kesler offers sensitive advice on coping with deparenting, adolescents, and everyday conflicts between parents and teenagers. He also discusses how most effectively to help teenagers who don't fit in with their peers because of "unaverage" size, being overweight, being physically handicapped, having severe acne, or being bereaved because of the loss of a friend or relative.

Mylander, Charles, *Running the Red Lights,* Ventura, CA: Regal Books, 1986.

The author tackles head-on the issues involved in sexual temptation and ways to keep a clean mind in a "dirty" world. Packed with scripture references, it deals with confronting someone who is sexually active in a caring manner, staying strong when emotions demand giving in to temptation, and seeking forgiveness after repentance.

Narramore, Bruce, *Why Children Misbehave,* Grand Rapids, MI: Zondervan, 1987.

Ever wonder why your sons aren't obedient and following in your steps? Narramore explores several reasons children misbehave: to gain control, to get attention, to seize power, or even for revenge. Appropriate strategies are given for dealing with children who are operating from these motives. You will be better able to discipline your sons if you understand why they are misbehaving.

Smith, Harold Ivan, *One Parent Families: Healing the Hurts,* Kansas City, MO: Beacon Hill, 1981.

This book, written by a divorced man, helps you understand and cope with the hurts of being a single parent.

Smith, Virginia Watts, *The Single Parent*, Old Tappan, NJ: Revell, 1977.

Virginia was widowed and found herself alone raising four children. How she not only survived but also found fulfillment as a single mother is inspirational reading.

Stewart, Suzanne, *Divorced!*, Grand Rapids, MI: Zondervan, 1974.

Suzanne's story is one of being left alone with three children to raise. With the Lord's help she was able to deal with guilt and anger in herself and abandonment in her children and to raise them to emotional and spiritual growth.

Stifford, Darrell, *Father and Son*, Philadelphia: Westminster Press, 1982.

Try this one for the father's perspective. Sometimes we get so involved in our feelings of being abandoned and having to raise sons alone that we may forget that there is another side to the story.

Weiss, Robert, *Going It Alone*, New York: Basic Books, 1979.

There is very little that can be said about single parenting that Robert Weiss has not said well in this book. He addresses the changes that occur when a family goes from being a two-parent situation to a one-parent home. His practical ideas for living successfully in a one-parent family are excellent. This book is full of research results but is highly readable and enjoyable.

White, John, *Parents in Pain,* Downers Grove, IL: InterVarsity Press, 1979.

Many parents face problems beyond their abilities to cope: alcoholism, homosexuality, suicide. Author John White not only gives some practical ideas on coping with such problems but also helps parents deal with their own guilt, frustration, anger, and sense of inadequacy.

Wilkerson, Rich, *Hold Me While You Let Me Go,* Irvine, CA: Harvest House, 1983.

Walking the road from childhood to adulthood with your sons will take a great deal of patience, maturity, and perseverance. Wilkerson gives pointers to parents on how to make the transition from parent to adviser and friend. Letting go too soon can mean failure for your sons. Letting go too late may result in a break in your relationship. Successful timing is more than guesswork, it is possible with prayer and sensitivity to your sons.